# MEDIT~~~~~ ~ ~ DIET FOR BEGINNERS

## The Complete Guide To Lose Weight And Live Healthier Following The Mediterranean Lifestyle

## ELIZABETH WELLS

# TABLE OF CONTENTS

# Free Bonus
## The Best Foods To Eat On A Ketogenic Diet

Discover the best foods to eat on a ketogenic diet. You'll learn the different food groups that you should eat to follow the keto diet correctly and start improving your health right now.

Go to **www.eepurl.com/cUqOlH** to download the guide for free.

# Introduction

Congratulations on purchasing your copy of the *Mediterranean Diet for Beginners: The Complete Guide To Lose Weight And Live Healthier Following The Mediterranean Lifestyle.* I am so excited that you have chosen to take a new path using the Mediterranean way of eating. Before we proceed, here's a bit of history:

Ancel Benjamin Keys, a scientist, and his colleagues including Paul Dudley White, which later became President Eisenhower's cardiac physician, conducted the 'Seven Countries Study' in the years following World War II comparing individuals in the United States to those living in Crete, a Mediterranean island. Keys examined the plan, testing people of all ages using the Mediterranean Diet.

The long-running study examined 13,000 middle-aged men, (remember the times), in the Netherlands, Yugoslavia, the United States, Finland, Greece, Italy, and Japan. It became evident the vegetables, fruits, beans, grains, and fish were the healthiest meals possible - even after the deprivations of WWII. All of these discoveries were just the starting point.

Many benefits will be discussed including how you can lose and maintain a healthy weight in a sustainable way. Each chapter will carry you through different aspects of the plan and guide you on how you can go about changing your eating patterns with the Mediterranean diet.

The fortunate part of the Mediterranean diet is that you don't have to travel to the exotic country to enjoy the cuisine. You can prepare the tasty meals with items from your cupboards and refrigerator using your stovetop, oven, and other appliances in your own home. You will also discover that, while on the Mediterranean diet plan, you will have more energy, and with that energy, you can become more active.

Motivation will be the leader you need to head towards your new lifestyle, making essential changes along the path to success. Now it's time to learn how to use the techniques of the Mediterranean diet plan.

# Chapter 1
## Basics of the Mediterranean Diet Plan

### How Weight Loss Works the Mediterranean Way

Your weight will depend on the amount energy your body burns and how much energy you consume from drink and food products. Simply stated

- If the ratio of the number of calories that you consume equals the amount your body is using, your weight will remain stable or unchanged.
- If you consume more food or calories than your body can utilize; you will gain weight. The excess or extra energy is converted to fat and is stored in your body.
- However, if you eat foods with more calories than your body can utilize, you'll lose the weight. It requires your body to tap into the stored body fat to obtain the additional energy needed.

By using the Mediterranean Diet plan, you can make sure that you are eating healthily. You need to pair it with physical activity. Therefore, to lose weight, you will need a calorie deficit. You can do this in two ways:

- Consume fewer calories from the food.
- Increase your physical activity, and use more calories

This is pretty much common sense, but there might be some rumors you may have heard.

## Here are the Myths of the Mediterranean Diet
## Myth 1

It is expensive to eat on this plan.

## Fact 1

The Mediterranean plan is not expensive if you are making the meals from lentils and beans for the protein source. You are also sticking with the whole grains and mostly plants which are much cheaper than processed or prepackaged food items.

## Myth 2

Have a huge bowl of pasta and bread; it is the Mediterranean way!

## Fact 2

Pasta is usually a side dish in the Mediterranean culture; they do not eat like the Americans. The helping is generally a portion of ½-cup to a 1-whole cup. Most of the meals consist of fish, vegetables, and salads; sometimes—a slice of bread or some grass-fed meat.

## Myth 3

The Mediterranean diet is just another food plan.

## Fact 3

The Mediterranean diet is a good food plan, but the plan helps in many other ways as have been indicated in this book. The food is made to be enjoyed while relaxing, which is equally important to your health as to what is on your plate.

## Myth 4

Three glasses of wine are great since one is good for your heart.

## Fact 4

The diet plan allows you to take red wine in moderation, which means two for men and one drink for women daily. Going over those limits can be damaging to your heart, health, and well-being.

# Chapter 2
## Portioning & the Shopping List

The first step is not to eat unless you are truly hungry. This section will first provide you with the essential groups of what to eat, drink, what to eat in moderation, what to eat rarely, and things you should avoid. You also need to know how many servings of what you are allowed based on the food pyramid of the Mediterranean Plan.

## Amount of Servings on the Mediterranean Pyramid

### Daily
- Water every day ** Plenty of it!
- Fruit ** 3
- Dairy Product ** 3
- Vegetables ** 6
- Olive Oil ** Acts as an added lipid
- Non-refined products and cereals ** 8 (whole-grain bread, brown rice, etc.)

## Weekly

- Eggs ** 3
- Sweets ** 3
- Nuts, Olives, Pulses ** 3-4
- Olive Oil ** 7-14 tbsp.
- Legumes ** 4
- Potatoes **3
- Poultry ** 4
- Fish ** 5-6

## Monthly

- Red Meat ** 4

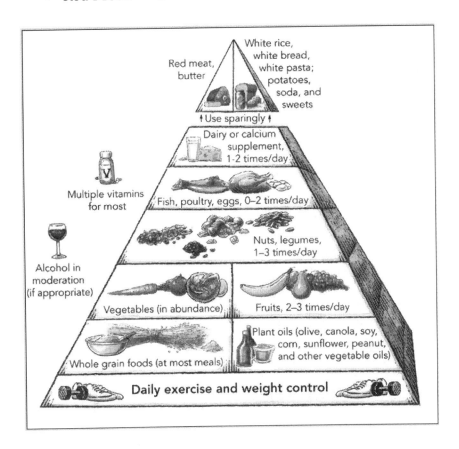

# Phase 1 - What You Should Eat & Drink – Explained

Maintaining a healthy body requires plenty of water. The World Health Organization (WHO) recommends you drink a minimum of eight to eleven cups of water each day if you are a woman, ten to fifteen if you are a man.

Tea and coffee are allowed, but avoid sugar-sweetened beverages and fruit juices that contain large amounts of sugar.

The diet plan allows about one glass (five ounces) of red wine for women. Men who are under 65 years of age are allowed two glasses daily for a total of ten ounces. However, men over 65 years old should have only one.

WHO also revealed millions of deaths annually are attributed to insufficient vegetable and fruit intake. Which is why they support the basis of the Mediterranean plan. Fruits, seeds, nuts, vegetables, spices, herbs, whole grains, seafood, fish, and the use of extra-virgin olive oil are some of the top items you want to eat.

These are some of the items in their groups:

## Spices and Herbs
Cinnamon, garlic, pepper, nutmeg, rosemary, sage, mint, basil, parsley, etc.

## Eggs
Duck, quail, and chicken eggs

## Fruits
Excellent choices for vitamin C, antioxidants, and fiber: Peaches, bananas, apples, figs, dates, pears,

oranges, strawberries, melons, grapes, etc.

## Dairy Products
Contain calcium, B12, and Vitamin A: Greek yogurt, regular yogurt, cheese, plus others

## Poultry
Turkey, duck, chicken, and more

## Vegetables
Excellent choices for fiber, and antioxidants: Cucumbers, carrots, Brussels sprouts, tomatoes, onions, broccoli, cauliflower, spinach, kale, eggplant, artichokes, fennel, etc.

## Seeds and Nuts
Provide minerals, vitamins, fiber, and protein: Macadamia nuts, cashews, pumpkin seeds, sunflower seeds, hazelnuts, chestnuts, Brazil nuts, walnuts, almonds, pumpkin seeds, sesame, poppy, and more

## Whole Grains
Whole-grain bread and pasta, buckwheat, whole-wheat, barley, corn, whole oats, rye, quinoa, bulgur, couscous, etc.

## Legumes
Provide vitamins, fiber, carbohydrates, and protein: Chickpeas, pulses, beans, lentils, peanuts, peas, etc.

## Tubers
Yams, turnips, potatoes, sweet potatoes, etc.

## Healthy Fats
Avocado oil, avocados, olives, extra virgin olive oil (EVOO)*Seafood and Fish*: Mussels, clams, crab, prawns, oysters, shrimp, tuna, mackerel, salmon,

trout, sardines, anchovies, and more

- ### What to Eat in Moderation
Poultry, eggs, milk, butter, yogurt, and cheese

- ### What to Eat Rarely
Red meats (Limit to once each week)

## Avoid these Groups

Added sugars, sugar-sweetened beverages, refined grains, processed meats and other highly processed foods. Out of this group, you will discover many foods such as these:

### Processed Meat Products

Hot dogs, processed sausages, bacon, and others

### Added Sugar

Ice cream, candies, table sugar, soda, and others

### Refined Grains

Pasta made with refined wheat, white bread, etc.

### Trans fats

Found in various processed foods such as margarine

### Refined Oils

Canola oil, Soybean oil, cottonseed oil, and several others

## Further Eating Restrictions: Phase Two
### Red Meats

You are allowed to consume red meats such as lamb, pork, and beef in small quantities. They are rich in minerals, vitamins, and protein—especially iron. Use caution because they do contain more fat—specifically saturated fat—compared to the fat content found in poultry. You don't have to eliminate it from your diet but try to enjoy your choice of red meats for a special dinner such as a casserole.

## White Meats
White meats are high in minerals, protein, and vitamins but you should remove any skin and fat.

## Potatoes
You receive potassium, Vitamin B, Vitamin C, and some of your daily fiber nutrients from potatoes. You need to be careful about how you use them because they contain large amounts of starch. That starch can be quickly converted to glucose which can be harmful and place you at risk of developing type 2 diabetes. Include potatoes in your diet by baking, boiling, and mashing them without butter.

## Desserts and Sweets
Biscuits, cakes, and sweets should be consumed in small quantities, as a special treat. Not only is the sugar a temptation for type 2 diabetes, but it can also promote tooth decay. Many times, they may also contain higher levels of saturated fats. You can receive some nutritional value, but as a general rule —stick to small portions.

# Some Healthy Simple Snacks

You should choose a healthy snack that's within the 150-200 calorie range. Choose an apple, grapefruit, or pear. Add a pinch (⅛ of a teaspoon) of sea salt for a change. This is a treat, but it will also fend off the hunger cravings. You want it to contain some whole-grain sources, some carbs, and protein to promote satiety.

These are just a few of the snacks you should

consider to beat the hunger pangs:

## Detox-Vegan Smoothie

You can pack in the nutrients and not use any animal products. Begin with some spirulina, a superfood type of algae, which will give the smoothie a pretty green color. Add some hemp protein powder to increase satiety with some almond milk, and frozen bananas. Add a sprig of mint and some chia seeds as a garnish to make it interesting.

## Fruit Slices and Nut Butter

A great way to challenge your sweet tooth is with some pears or apples and a dip of nut butter. Almond and cashew butter are superb options which contain heart-healthy fats. It is as simple as roasting and blending a few raw almonds to achieve the healthy fiber and protein-rich snack food.

## Dates and Figs

These are some products which grow well in the Mediterranean climate. They are also a sweet treat when you are too busy to prepare a snack.

## Greek Yogurt and Fruit

Enjoy a protein-rich snack of some Greek yogurt (it doesn't come from Greece). Garnish the yogurt with some sunflower seeds, a handful of berries, and a drizzle of honey for a tasty mid-afternoon snack.

## Pita and Hummus

You can have some sesame paste (tahini) and chickpeas in the form of hummus. Consider making some at home, but you can also purchase it ready-made. Make sure you read the label and choose one with a limited amount of preservatives. You can choose a whole-wheat piece of pita bread with a hummus spread for a delicious snack.

## Tuna Salad and Crackers

It is time to move away from the traditional tuna salad. Substitute oil-packed tuna with a splash of red vinegar wine, scallions, and a squeeze of mustard. Add some whole wheat crackers for a mid-morning treat.

## Kalamata Olives

When you are in a rush, nothing says it all like a handful of healthy olives. They are rich in many antioxidants including oleic acid, tyrosol, and hydroxytyrosol. Mix them up with a small amount of feta cheese for an additional boost.

# Substitute "This for That"

### Instead of a Hot Dog – Try Canned Fish

Inflammation and preventive brain cognitive decline are provided by fatty fish (high in omega-3s). Stock up if you are on a budget for the time you need a quick lunch or snack. Forget about the hot dog, since it is loaded with additives, preservatives, and chemicals that can induce an inflammatory response in your body.

### Forget the Chips and Try Nuts Instead

The Mediterranean Diet includes the nuts which provide the fat and protein to put it high above on the satiety index. However, other than fending off the hunger; there is also a bigger benefit. It helps lower the cholesterol whereas the chips are considered 'empty' calories with a layer of salt.

### Purchase Whole Grain Bread - Not White

White bread is devoid of nutrients since it is made from overly-processed refined flour. White can also induce weight gain. It can also cause spikes in blood sugar which will cause you to get hungry more easily as well as gain weight. Whole grains are full of fiber and energy-boosting B vitamins. Consider bread such as Ezekiel for your avocado toast and sandwiches.

## Portion Guidelines

These are some general guidelines so you can better calculate the serving sizes for your meal planning needs:

### Dairy

One cup of yogurt or one cup of milk, 30 grams or about 1.1 ounces of cheese

### Eggs

One egg

### Fruit

One orange, one apple, one banana, 30 grams: 1.1 ounces of grapes: 7.1 ounces of watermelon or other melons

### Grains

50 to 60 grams (1/2 cup) of cooked rice or pasta: One slice of bread is 25 grams (almost an ounce)

### Nuts

30 grams (1.1 ounces) Sprinkled on foods for flavor or as a snack

### Legumes

100 grams (One cup) of dry cooked beans

### Meat

60 grams (2.1 ounces) of fish or lean meat

### Potatoes

100 grams (3.5 ounces)

**Vegetables**
One cup of raw leafy veggies or one-half cup of all others

**Wine**
125 ml or about a 4.2-ounce glass of a regular strength red wine

# Consider Replacements and Make Substitutes

- Eliminate butter and use canola or olive oil.
- Stop using salt and rely on spices and herbs.
- Switch to whole grains.
- Leave the red meat and substitute with some poultry or fish.
- Choose natural peanut butter and leave the hydrogenated fat on the shelf. Try using tahini as a spread or a dip.
- Switch to a low-fat cheese or 2% milk and move away from the higher fat products.
- Make some pudding with skim or whole milk instead of ice cream.
- Use sandwich fillings using whole wheat tortillas versus a sandwich made with rolls or white bread.
- Make some quinoa with a dish of stir-fried veggies instead of the stir-fry with rice.

## The Basic Shopping List

It is always best to have the healthiest options available when you want to prepare a meal using the guidelines provided on the Mediterranean Diet Plan.

This is a general list for your convenience:

## Frozen Products
- Vegetables of your Choice
- Shrimp
- Berries

## Dairy and Cheese
- Greek Yogurt
- Eggs
- Cheese of your Choice

## Healthy Fats
- Avocados
- Extra-virgin olive oil (EVOO)
- Favorite Seeds and nuts

## Legumes and Canned Beans
- Lentils
- Garbanzo
- Black
- White
- Kidney

## Meat and Seafood
- Lean Pork
- Chicken
- Salmon

## Whole Grains
- Quinoa
- Whole Grain Pasta
- Farro

## Unlimited—Your Favorites
- Fresh Vegetables
- Herbs
- Spices

# Beyond the Basics

Now that you understand the basic shopping list for the Mediterranean Diet, you need to become more precise and improve your list by using these specific food groups.

## Poultry and Eggs
- Duck
- Chicken
- Guinea fowl

## Dairy Products
- Plain yogurt
- Fat-free sour cream or fat-free half-and-half
- Shredded strong cheeses (ex. Asiago, ricotta, brie, feta, etc.)
- Fat-free milk, hemp or rice milk, soy milk, or almond milk

## Fruits, Unsweetened apples, and bananas
- Melons
- Pineapple
- Apricots
- Strawberries
- Applesauce
- Cherries
- Nectarines
- Dates
- Peaches
- Figs
- Pears
- Mango
- Grapes

## Lean Protein
- Nuts like dry-roasted and unsalted almonds, pistachios, nut butter, and walnuts
- Egg Substitutes
- Shellfish/Fish: Halibut, tuna, salmon, flounder, shrimp, abalone, eel, crab, lobster, mackerel, octopus, sardines, squid, whelk, yellowtail, sea bass
- Peas, beans, and lentils (frozen with no additives) or (canned if rinsed)
- Vegetarian Proteins: Tempeh, tofu, etc.

## Fats and Oils
- Spray oils
- Extra-virgin olive oil
- Canola oil

## Seasonings and Spices
- Fresh Herbs: dill rosemary, basil mint, parsley, etc.
- Whole or minced garlic
- Lime, lemon
- Anise
- Bay Leaf
- Chiles
- Clove
- Cumin
- Capers
- Mustards
- Horseradish
- Aged balsamic vinegar
- Pepper
- Thyme
- Tarragon
- Many other low-sodium blends or seasonings

## Cereals
- Unsweetened shredded wheat
- Steel-cut oatmeal or quick-cooking

## Grains, Bread, and Pasta
- 100% whole-wheat bread
- Whole-wheat pasta products
- Quinoa
- Barley
- Buckwheat
- Bulgur
- Millet
- Oats Polenta
- Wheat berries
- Brown Rice
- Whole grain couscous

## Vegetables and Tubers
- Broccoli
- Onions (red, white, sweet), chives, shallots
- Tomatoes
- Dark Green Veggies
- Artichokes
- Asparagus
- Beets
- Brussels Sprouts
- Celery
- Collards
- Chicory
- Cucumbers
- Carrots
- Dandelion Greens
- Dark Green Veggies
- Roasted Bell Peppers

- Cabbage
- Peas
- Potatoes
- Sweet Potatoes
- Pumpkin
- Purslane
- Radishes
- Rutabaga
- Eggplant
- Spinach
- Turnips
- Zucchini

**Chocolate and Wine**
- Chocolate Bars: A minimum of 60% dark cacao (not processed with alkali)
- Unsweetened dark cocoa powder
- Cabernet Sauvignon, Pinot Noir

This list of products should be all you need to get your Mediterranean home routine started. Of course, once you get the routine, it will not be like a diet, it will be a new lifestyle.

# Consider Switching to Olive Oil

The monosaturated fat which is found in olive oil is a fat that can help reduce low-density lipoprotein cholesterol (LDL-C) or also known as a bad cholesterol. This oil has become the traditional fat worldwide with some of the healthiest populations. A great deal of research has been provided showing the oil is a huge plus in avoiding the risks of heart disease because of the antioxidants and fatty acids it contains.

You will still need to pay close attention when

purchasing olive oil because it may not have been extracted from the olives using chemicals or possibly diluted with other cheaper oils, such as canola and soybean. You need to be aware of refined oil, light olive or regular oils.

The Mediterranean diet plan calls for the use of extra-virgin olive oil because it has been standardized for purity using natural methods providing the highest qualities of its excellent taste and smell. The oil is high in phenolic antioxidants which makes—real—olive oil beneficial.

These are some of the nutrients contained in extra-virgin olive oil based on 100 grams (about 3.4 ounces):

- Monosaturated Fat: 73% (the 18 carbon long oleic acid)
- Saturated Fat: 13.8%
- Omega-3: 0.76%
- Omega-6: 9.7%
- Vitamin E is 72% of the RDA
- Vitamin K is 75% of the RDA

*Note*: RDA stands for the recommended dietary allowance or the recommended daily allowance. It is the number of nutrients necessary daily for the maintenance of your good health calculated by the Food and Nutrition Board of the National Research Council.

## Recipes and Balance with the Meal Plan

There are so many delicious ways you can savor the Mediterranean way of eating. This chapter will provide you with specific information on how you should begin your new journey to a better life.

## How to Balance Out the Plan

- Always eat breakfast. Make a new habit or continue to have a fiber-rich breakfast consisting of whole grains and fruits to get your day going.
- Eat cereals and whole grain bread with your meals.
- Save sweet drinks and other special sweet treats for special occasions.
- Choose yogurt daily as a snack or dessert.
- Cheese should be limited to approximately one ounce or no more than an ounce and a half (30 to 40 grams each day). Consider eating natural cheese, raw milk or organic dairy products.
- Eat a minimum of two legume-based meals each week.
- Reserve one night of the week just for veggies. You could begin a routine of making Fridays 'Meatless Friday' by planning a meal around whole grains, beans, and vegetables. You can also eat a vegetable with every meal like 3 ½-ounces each of tomatoes, leafy greens and about 7-ounces of other veggies.
- Eat nuts, fruit, or dried fruit as a dessert or as a snack.
- Consume minimal portions of meat; no more than one or two times weekly.
- You should consume seafood and freshly-caught fish at least two times each week.
- Most recipes have plenty of salt when they are cooked. Don't add extra salt at the table. It is probably a good idea to remove the temptation and place the shaker in the kitchen.

The plan also involves receiving the most enjoyment out of life, along with regular physical activities. You will figure it out by making the healthy choices and eating the broccoli, celery, carrots, and salsa instead of a bowl of ranch dip with crackers, chips, or crackers. There are so many ways you can improve your diet. It just takes a lot of determination and a bit of planning.

# **Chapter 3**
## Health Benefits

The Mediterranean Diet plan is built on healthy fats as well as plant-based foods. Since the plan does not eliminate entire food groups, it is believed you should not have any problems complying with it in the long term.

After extensive research, these are some of the health benefits which you can gain from following the diet:

### Fact 1: Agility Improves
Studies have shown up to 70% of the seniors who are at risk of developing frailty or other muscle weaknesses have reduced the risk factors using the plan.

*The Journal of the American Medical Association'* discovered a 60% reduction when exercise was added to the diet.

### Fact 2: Vision Improvements
You might be able to stave off –or even prevent –the risk of macular degeneration which is the major cause for adults over 54 losing their eyesight. The

condition affects over ten million Americans and can destroy the area of your retina, the part of your eye responsible for clear vision. Vegetables and fish that contain plenty of omega-3 fatty acids are the best choices to lower or reduce the risk entirely. Also, you will have less chance of developing cataracts with the consumption of green leafy veggies that contain lutein.

## Fact 3: A Diet Low in Sugar and Processed Foods

You can certainly appreciate a diet or a way of life that is close to nature, especially if you can locate some locally produced organic food. People in the Mediterranean enjoy the same kinds of delicious desserts, but many are made using natural sweeteners such as honey.

## Fact 4: Lose Weight in a Healthy Way

Your search is over if you are seeking a plan that is worthwhile. The Mediterranean Diet plan has been proven to be effective in helping lose weight naturally with its many nutrient-dense foods. The focus is placed on healthy fats to keep the carbs moderately low and improve overall health by adding high-quality proteins.

Now, you may wonder how you can lose weight with a diet which is high in fat. The healthy fats, protein, and fiber keep you much more satisfied than candy, chips, or cookies. The veggies make up the bulk of the meal by filling your stomach, so you don't feel hungry an hour after your meal, and you won't receive a spike your blood sugar.

## Fact 5: Lowered Risk of Heart Disease and Strokes

Patients who used the plan experienced a lower

level of oxidized low-density lipoprotein or LDL cholesterol. This is the bad cholesterol that can build up in your arteries.

The Mediterranean diet is rich in alpha-linolenic acid (ALA), that is found in extra-virgin olive oil. The 'Warwick Medical School' involved participants in a study where they were divided into two groups: those who consumed more EVOO versus those who consumed sunflower oil. The results showed that the participants who took olive oil were positive for decreased blood pressure.

Lowered hypertension is another benefit achieved by consuming olive oil because it helps keep the arteries clear and dilated. It makes the nitric oxide more bioavailable. The healthy fats also make you less likely to struggle with maintaining low cholesterol levels.

Strokes can be caused by bleeding in the brain or a blocked blood vessel. You may notice numbness, weakness, headaches, confusion, vision problems, dizziness or slurred speech. The diet helps with these issues.

## Fact 6: Asthma Symptoms are Reduced by the Plan
Numerous studies have revealed that the diet helped children who followed the plan, emphasizing the intake of plant-based foods and lower intake of red meats.

## Fact 7: Relaxation and De-stressing
One thing that happens in the Mediterranean that is usually not as evident in the United States is the love of outdoors and nature. The keyword is 'active.' Bonding with good friends, family, and eating

delicious healthy food is a superb stress reliever. It has been discovered that red wine in moderation is one way to fight obesity, among other benefits.

## Fact 8: Metabolic Complications of Obesity
These are just a few: Raised blood pressure, low HDL cholesterol heart disease, high triglycerides, belly fat, etc.

## Fact 9: Diabetes Prevention and Treatment
The Mediterranean Diet controls excessive insulin, which is a hormone that controls your blood sugar levels and can cause you to gain weight and keep it on, no matter what you try to lose it.

The well-balanced diet makes use of carbs which are low in sugar and contains healthy fatty acids that can help your body burn off the fat faster and give you more energy at the same time.

The diet is considered lower in saturated fat, but higher in fat than the American standard diet plans, according to the 'American Heart Association.' The combination is usually 20-30% quality protein foods, 30-40% healthy fats, and 40% complex carbs. This creates the balance to keep your hunger under control and help keep the weight gain down which is an excellent way to keep insulin levels normalized.

As a result, with the energy levels up—so should your mood. The only sugar usually consumed through dessert, fruit, or wine. The balance also prevents the 'highs and lows' which is the mood-altering factor.

Most individuals on the plan will eat a balanced breakfast within one or two hours from the time the day starts, which is the time of day where the lowest levels of blood sugar are present in the healthy fats and fibers, along with three meals each day to maintain the balance.

## Fact 10: Parkinson's Risk Factors are Reduced

The risk of the disease is cut in half because the high levels of antioxidants in the diet prevent oxidative stress, the process where cells are damaged as a result.

Parkinson's disease affects the cells in your brain that produce dopamine. You may have some issues with gait and speech patterns, tremors, and muscle rigidity issues.

## Fact 11: Alzheimer's Risk factors are Reduced

The Mediterranean diet can help safeguard you from Alzheimer's a condition characterized by thinking, judgment, and memory loss. Research has deemed a 40% reduction occurs for those who use the diet plan, and the risk factors associated with Alzheimer's.

Dementia may progress in the later stages of Alzheimer's which can be treated with medication and aided by the Mediterranean diet plan. You should also consider some additional exercise to slow the process.

These are just some of the benefits, but now we can move on and dine out!

# Chapter 4
## Dining Out

Never feel like you cannot go out with friends and still have an enjoyable – healthy meal. Most restaurants are a reasonable choice for you while you are participating in this diet plan.

## Restaurant Options

Here are some suggestions when making a request

- Ask the waiter or waitress to cook your food using extra-virgin olive oil (EVOO) instead of butter.
- Choose to have a house salad and extra veggies.
- Have some seafood or other types of fish for the main entree.
- Eat whole-grain bread.

Many of the restaurants are willing to alter the dishes offered on the menu to meet specific dietary needs. You could always request a pink sauce for a dish that may normally have a sauce such as Alfredo in it. You could also request the regular marinara sauce. One of the diet's advantages is that it's very flexible.

# Additional Tips for the Restaurant

## Appetizers
- Share your appetizer, so you will have a smaller portion or you can skip it.
- Don't give in to the temptation and ask the waiter or waitress to bring a bread-and-butter basket to the table. If you are hungry, you may be tempted to eat more than you should.
- Avoid fried appetizers. Stick with some steamed fish or shellfish, mixed salads, broth-based soups, or grilled veggies.

## Entrees
- Choose from lean pork (center-cut or tenderloin), fish, poultry, or vegetarian choices.If you are bound for red meat—choose the leaner cuts such as flank, sirloin, filet mignon, or a tenderloin. You might also want to consider that beef will have a higher calorie and higher fat count.
- Use caution with sauces. Ask if it is oil based, or if there's cream or butter in the sauce. Avoid sauces with cream, cheese, oil, or butter. Request that the sauces to be in a separate container, so you can add what is allowed. Use your fork to dip the sauce and limit the temptation of over-indulging.
- Ask for substitutes for mashed potatoes, macaroni salad, potato salad, coleslaw or french fries. Instead, choose a side salad, steamed rice, baked potato, or the good side dish, steamed veggies.
- Eat only half of the portion or share it with a friend. You can always ask for 'doggie bag' and enjoy the leftovers later. It will be an excellent lunch meal. You can also ask for half of the

meal to be held in the kitchen until you are through with your meal. Once again, resist the temptation!

- Enjoy your meal and eat slowly. Ask to have the plate removed when you feel full.

## Beverages

- Have a non-caloric beverage like tea, seltzer water, water, sugar-free or diet soda. Choose a splash or orange juice or cranberry juice in some seltzer water for a fizzy surprise.
- If you decide on alcohol, remember the limitations, and keep score. A one-ounce shot, a 12-ounce light beer, and a six-ounce glass of wine are 120 calories each. You also have to remember the general rule of one beverage for women and two beverages for healthy men.

## Desserts

Try these ideas:

- Have a cup of coffee, cappuccino, or some herbal tea with a sugar substitute or no sugar with some skim milk.
- Order some berries or mixed fruit.
- Order a dessert for everyone at the table to enjoy.

# Restaurant Choices & Guidelines

You now know some of your choices but here are some extra tips for several restaurants to make your dieting plan even easier at Subway, Taco Bell, Wendy's, Kentucky Fried Chicken (KFC), Burger King, and McDonald's which offer you a healthier choice. As with any other meal, when in doubt— leave it out!

## Burger King
Some of the healthy dishes include

- BK Veggie Burger: The sandwich has low-fat content, so you can remove or use the mayonnaise.
- Chicken Whopper: No cheese and skip the mayo.
- Several salads are offered: Fire Grilled Chicken or Shrimp Garden Salad, and Shrimp Caesar.

## McDonald's
These are some of the healthy choices you will find at McDonald's:

- Breakfast offers Apple Dippers with a low-fat caramel dip or a yogurt parfait.
- Caesar Salad with Grilled Chicken
- Bacon Ranch Salad with Grilled Chicken
- Chicken Mc-Grill Sandwich: Leave off the mayonnaise and cheese.
- McChicken Patty: Do not add the cheese or the mayo.

## Subway
This is one place where you can really choose your

diet. After all, eating fresh is their motto. You can choose any 6-inch sub with the following ingredients:

- Savory Turkey Breast
- Subway Club
- Savory Turkey Breast and Ham
- Oven Roasted Chicken Breast
- Ham
- Honey Mustard Ham
- Sweet Onion Chicken Teriyaki
- Roast Beef

You can choose from different kinds bread - wheat or Italian, and a variety of veggies to keep them under the six grams of fat. Just leave the cheese off of the tasty sandwich.

Choose one of these salads under the same six grams of fat:

- Subway Club Salad
- Savory Turkey Breast and Ham Salad
- Savory Turkey Breast Salad
- Grilled Chicken Breast Strips Salad
- Grilled Chicken Breast Strips Baby Spinach Salad

You can even splurge with some croutons since these salads are so low on the calorie counts. You can use a fat-free salad dressing (Italian). You could always take your own Lite Mediterranean Vinaigrette for the dressing to be sure you have one to stay with the plan.

## KFC

You can enjoy oven roasted chicken strip meals, but

you won't get to add the sides if you choose this meal. They also offer side dishes like seasoned rice, BBQ baked beans, green beans, a small corn on the cob or some applesauce for dessert. They also offer some excellent combos with the sides menu to better suit your budget and diet!

## Taco Bell

You can cut the fats in your food by 25% if you order any of these items using the Fresco style which will replace the cheese or any sauce:

- Enchirito Steak or Chicken
- Tostada
- Fiesta Burrito Chicken
- Gordita Baja Steak or Chicken
- Bean Burrito
- Burrito Supreme Chicken or Steak
- Ranchero Chicken Soft Taco
- Grilled Steak or Chicken Soft Taco

## Wendy's

These are a few of the tasty meal choices offered with sufficient choices to complement your diet plans:

- Baked Potato: You can add some chili, broccoli, or chives. Leave the bacon and cheese off of the potato.
- Ultimate Chicken Grill: Just leave off the creamy sauce, mayonnaise, cheese, and bacon.
- Large Chili: Omit the shredded cheese.
- Spring Mix Salad: Leave off the bacon and pecans.
- Mandarin Chicken Salad: Use the rice noodles but skip the almonds.
- Jr. Hamburger: Have a plain potato and a side salad.

# Chapter 5
## The 14-Day Meal Plan

You now have some of the information necessary to get your health back in line and feel better in the process. This chapter will provide you with some basic guidelines that will be useful for your continued success with the Mediterranean diet plan. Try out some of the tempting recipes for breakfast, lunch, and dinner. Each of the recipes contained in this book is delicious. You can switch it around to suit your schedule; it is so flexible!

## Day 1

**Breakfast -** Blueberry Almond Smoothie
**Lunch** - Tasty Gyros with Tzatziki Sauce
**Dinner -** Broiled Salmon
**Sides -**Brussels Sprouts With Honey Pomegranate and Apples

## Day 2

**Breakfast -** Mediterranean Breakfast Quinoa
**Lunch -** Bento Lunchtime Delight

**Dinner -** Stuffed Peppers
**Snack-time -** Picnic Snack

# Day 3

**Brunch -** Avocado Egg Salad
**Dinner -** Chickpea Patties
**Side Dish -** Greek Salad & Avocado
**Snack or Appetizer:** Basil & Tomato Finger Sandwiches

# Day 4

**Breakfast -** Almond Biscotti
**Lunch –** Shrimp Salad Cucumber Cups
**Dinner -** Lemony Salmon & Lima Beans
**Snack or Dessert -** Cherries – Toasted Almonds and Ricotta

# Day 5

**Breakfast -** Blueberry Fields Smoothie
**Lunch -** Mediterranean Chicken Quinoa Bowl – 3 oz. chicken – ½ c. quinoa & ¼ c. of the sauce
**Dinner -** Lamb Lettuce Wraps
**Side:** Grilled Zucchini – Tomato & Feta
**Snack or Dessert -** Cranberry, Goat Cheese, and Walnut Canapés

# Day 6

**Breakfast –** Shakshuka with Feta - Skillet Dish
**Lunch -** Mediterranean Tuna
**Dinner -** Lemon - Za'atar -Grilled Chicken
**Side Dish -** Mediterranean Bean Salad

# Day 7

**Breakfast** - "Egg-cetera"
**Lunch** - Greek Kale Salad with Quinoa Chicken
**Dinner** - Rigatoni with Asiago Cheese & Green Olive-Almond Pesto
**Sides or Snack** - Marinated Olives & Feta
**Dessert** - Creamy Blueberries

# Day 8

**Breakfast** - Greek Yogurt Pancakes
**Lunch** - Lemon & Egg Greek Soup
**Dinner** - Grilled Lamb with Mint Tomato Quinoa
**Snack or Appetizer** - Date Wraps

# Day 9

**Breakfast** - Cucumber Spinach Smoothie
**Lunch** - Balsamic Berry Vinaigrette Winter Salad
**Dinner** - Lamb with Garlic & Rosemary

# Day 10

**Breakfast** - Greek Egg Frittata
**Lunch** - Mediterranean Tuna Antipasto Salad
**Dinner** - Spicy Spinach Lentil Soup
**Snack or Dessert** - Greek Yogurt Parfait

# Day 11

**Breakfast** - Scrambled Eggs with Spinach – Tomato & Feta
**Lunch** - Vegan Buddha Bowl

**Dinner –** Hassel-back Caprese Chicken
**Sides** - Herbed Mashed Potatoes with Greek Yogurt

## Day 12

**Breakfast** - Peaches – Ricotta & Thyme Honey
**Lunch** - Creamy Mediterranean Panini
**Dinner** - Salmon Rice Bowl
**Snack or Appetizer** - Cucumber Roll-Ups

## Day 13

**Breakfast** - Honey Caramelized Figs & Yogurt
**Lunch** - Greek Orzo Salad
**Dinner** - Seared Tuna Steaks
**Sides** - Tomato & Basil Skewers

## Day 14

**Breakfast** - Potato Hash and Chickpeas
**Lunch** - Shrimp Scampi
**Sides** - Herbed Olives
**Dinner –** Grilled Chicken & Roasted Pepper Panini
**Sides** - Broccoli – Chickpea & Pomegranate Salad

Now you have the plan; next are the recipes so you
can learn how to make each one!

# Chapter 6
## Breakfast & Brunch Delights

## Almond Biscotti

Makes 4-6 Servings - varies

*Ingredients*
- 1 lb. flour
- 1 lb. lightly toasted whole almonds
- 4 eggs (+) 1 egg
- 2 t. vanilla
- Zest of 2 lemons
- 1 t. baking powder
- ½ lb. sugar

*Directions*
1. Program the oven temperature to 350ºF. Prepare a cookie sheet with parchment paper. Slice the almonds in half.
2. Mix four of the eggs and the remainder of ingredients in a large mixing bowl.
3. Process the dough into a 1 ½-inch thickness making three logs and place on the prepared baking sheet. Beat and spread the last egg over the logs and bake for 30 minutes.
4. When it is ready, cut the logs into ½-inch wide slices. Place it back in the oven at 300ºF for 25 more minutes.

## Avocado Egg Salad
Makes 4 Servings

*Ingredients*
- Salt to taste
- 1 tbsp. lemon juice
- 2 hard-boiled eggs
- 3 green onions
- 1 avocado
- 3 tbsp. boiled corn
- 1 tbsp. olive oil
- 1 thinly chopped tomato

*Directions*
1. Chop the green onions.
2. Blend the lemon juice and the finely chopped avocado in a large mixing container.
3. Mix the remainder of the components in the mixture (leave the tomato).
4. Serve with chopped tomatoes on bread slices.

# Greek Yogurt Pancakes

Makes 9-11 medium pancakes

*Ingredients*
- 4 tbsp. milk
- 2 large eggs.
- 2/3 c. vanilla Greek yogurt
- 1 t. baking powder
- ¾ c. all-purpose flour
- For sautéing: Butter/olive or coconut oil

*Directions*
1. Whisk the yogurt, milk, and eggs together.
2. Combine the baking powder and flour and blend in with the mixture. Add more milk if needed.
3. Melt or warm the oil of choice over medium heat. Spend about two minutes per side.

## Peaches - Ricotta & Thyme Honey
Makes 1-2 Servings - varies

*Ingredients*
- 2 small peaches or 1 large nectarine per person
- Crumbly ricotta
- Honey
- Fresh mint/ thyme sprig
- Pistachios/another favorite nut
- Sprinkle - caster sugar for peaches

*Directions*
1. Warm up a cast iron pan. Wash and dry the peaches then slice into halves.
2. Sprinkle with the sugar and add to the warm pan until seared.
3. Cool and serve with some thick yogurt or a dollop of ricotta.
4. Sprinkle with the nuts, sprigs of mint or thyme, and a drizzle of honey.

## Potato Hash and Chickpeas
Makes 4 Servings

*Ingredients*
- 1 can (15 oz.) chickpeas
- ½ c. onion
- 1 c. zucchini
- 2 c. baby spinach
- 4 c. hash brown potatoes - frozen & shredded
- 1 tbsp. each
  - Curry powder
  - Freshly minced ginger
- ¼ c. olive oil
- ½ t. salt
- 4 large eggs

*Directions*
1. Rinse the chickpeas thoroughly and chop the zucchini. Finely chop the onion and baby spinach. Mix the onion, spinach, potatoes, salt, ginger, and curry powder in a large mixing bowl.
2. Using medium-high heat, prepare a large skillet with the oil. Combine the potato mixture, and cook without stirring for about three to five minutes pressing it into a layer. Reduce the heat to medium-low. Mix in the zucchini and chickpeas, while breaking up the potatoes. Press into an even layer once again.
3. In the center, carve out four wells or holes, while one at a time you place an egg into the slot.
4. Use a top to cover the pan, continuing to cook for another four to five minutes to make a soft yolk.

## Egg-cetera
Makes 4 Servings

*Ingredients*
- 4 hard-boiled eggs
- ½ t. of each:
  - Kosher salt
  - Paprika
- 1 t. extra-virgin olive oil

*Directions*
1. Prepare the eggs by arranging them in a single layer in a saucepan then fill it with water. Use the medium heat setting to bring it to a simmer. Reduce to low heat for 10 minutes then remove from the hot water. Prepare a cold-water bath until cooled. Peel the eggs and slice.
2. Dip the eggs in the oil and sprinkle with the paprika and salt as desired.

## Greek Egg Frittata
Makes 6 Servings

*Ingredients*
- 6 eggs
- ½ c. of each:
    - Cream/milk
    - Diced tomatoes
- ¼ c. chopped of each:
    - Spanish olives
    - Kalamata olives
- 1 c. chopped spinach
- ¼ c. crumbled feta
- ½ t. pepper
- 1 t. of each:
    - Oregano
    - Salt
- Also Needed: Quiche pan or 8-inch pie pan

*Directions*
1. Set the oven's temperature to 400ºF. Grease the baking pan.
2. Whisk the milk and eggs and add the rest of the ingredients. Mix well.
3. Bake until the eggs are set, usually about 15-20 minutes.

# Honey Caramelized Figs & Yogurt
Makes 4 Servings

*Ingredients*
- 1 tbsp. (+) more honey for drizzling
- 8 oz. fresh figs – halved
- 2 c. plain Greek yogurt - low-fat
- ¼ c. chopped pistachios
- Pinch - cinnamon

*Directions*
1. Heat the honey in a pan using the medium-high heat setting on the stovetop.
2. Add the figs – cut side down – and simmer until caramelized, usually about five minutes.
3. Have several with a dish of yogurt, pistachios, a drizzle of honey, and a little cinnamon.

# Mediterranean Breakfast Quinoa

Makes 2-3 Servings

*Ingredients*
- 1 c. quinoa
- ¼ c. chopped raw almonds
- 5 dried apricots
- 1 t. ground cinnamon
- 2 dried pitted dates
- 2 tbsp. honey
- 1 t. sea salt
- 2 c. milk
- 1 t. vanilla extract

*Directions*
1. Finely chop the dates and apricots.
2. Over medium heat, toast the almonds three to five minutes in a skillet. Set to the side.
3. Heat the quinoa, salt, and cinnamon using medium heat until warm. Pour in the milk. When the mixture boils, reduce the heat, and place a lid on the saucepan, continue cooking slowly for approximately 15 minutes.
4. Pour in the honey, vanilla, apricots, dates, and half of the almonds.
5. Garnish with the rest of the almonds. Serve!

# Scrambled Eggs with Spinach – Tomato & Feta
Makes 1-2 Servings

*Ingredients*
- 1/3 c. tomato – approx. ½ med. tomato
- 1 tbsp. vegetable oil
- 1 c. baby spinach
- 3 eggs
- Pepper and salt to taste
- 2 tbsp. feta cheese

*Directions*
1. Remove the seeds and dice the tomatoes. Cut the feta into cubes.
2. Warm up a skillet using medium heat. Saute the spinach and tomatoes.
3. When the spinach is wilted, add the eggs. Scramble until done and give it a shake of salt and pepper.

## Shakshuka with Feta - Skillet Dish
Makes 6 Servings

*Ingredients*
- 1 jalapeno chili pepper
- 1 large of each:
  - Onion
  - Sweet pepper
- 3 cloves of garlic
- 2 tbsp. olive oil
- ½ t. kosher salt
- 1 t. of each:
  - Ground turmeric
  - Ground cumin
  - Sweet paprika
- ¼ t. black pepper
- 1 can (28 oz.) whole plum tomatoes with juices
- 6 eggs
- Feta cheese
- For the Garnish: Oregano & Fresh cilantro

*Directions*
1. Chop the peppers, onion, and jalapeno (seeds removed). Coarsely chop the tomatoes.
2. Heat up the oil (med.) in a large skillet. Toss in the peppers, onion, jalapeno, garlic, paprika, cumin, pepper, salt, and turmeric.
3. Cook for about ten minutes. Mix in the tomatoes with juices. Once it starts to boil, just lower the heat and continue cooking slowly for ten minutes. Stir occasionally.
4. Add one egg at a time into a bowl and gently add over the sauce. Cover and lower the heat. Cook for about five to ten minutes.
5. Top with the feta and other garnishes. Tasty!

# Smoothies

## Blueberry Almond Smoothie
Makes 2 Servings

*Ingredients*
- 16 oz. unsweetened almond milk
- 4 oz. heavy cream
- Stevia to taste
- 1 scoop whey vanilla isolate powder
- ¼ c. frozen unsweetened blueberries

*Directions*
1. Pour the milk along with the rest of the ingredients in a blender.
2. Blend until the mixture smoothens. Serve it up in a couple of chilled glasses.

## Blueberry Fields

Makes 1 Serving

*Ingredients*
- 1 c. coconut milk
- ¼ c. blueberries
- 1 t. of each:
    - Vanilla Essence
    - MCT Oil
- 1 scoop Whey protein powder – optional


*Directions*
1. For a quick burst of energy, add all of the ingredients in a blender.
2. Puree until it reaches the desired consistency. Add some ice if you wish.

## Cucumber Spinach Smoothie

Makes 1 Serving

*Ingredients*
- 2 ½ oz. cucumber
- 2 handfuls of spinach
- 1 c. coconut milk – carton
- ¼ t. xanthan gum
- 12 drops liquid stevia
- 1-2 tbsp. MCT oil
- 7 large cubes of ice

*Directions*
1. Peel and cut the cucumber into cubes. Add it, and the remainder of the ingredients in a blender.
2. Puree the mixture for one to two minutes.
3. Serve in a chilled glass.

# Chapter 7
## Lunchtime Specialties

### Bento Lunchtime Delight
Makes 1 Serving

*Ingredients*
- ¼ c. of each:
  - Diced tomato
  - Rinsed chickpeas
  - Diced cucumber
- 1 tbsp. of each:
  - Diced olives
  - Feta cheese – crumbled
  - Freshly chopped parsley
- ½ t. EVOO
- 1 c. grapes
- 1 t. red wine vinegar
- 3 oz. grilled chicken/turkey breast
- 1 – quartered – whole wheat pita bread
- 2 tbsp. hummus

*Directions*
1. Combine the tomatoes, chickpeas, olives, cucumber, parsley, feta, vinegar, and olive oil in a medium container.
2. In another container add the chicken and another for the hummus dip.
3. Pack-and-Go anytime!

## Creamy Mediterranean Panini
Makes 4 Servings

*Ingredients*
- ½ c. mayonnaise - divided
- 2 tbsp. oil-cured black olives
- ¼ c. basil leaves
- 8 slices bread (½-in. thick whole-grain)
- 1 small zucchini
- 4 slices provolone cheese
- 1 jar roasted (7 oz.) red peppers

*Directions*
1. Drain and slice the peppers. Finely chop the olives and cut the zucchini into thin slices.
2. Combine the oil and ¼ cup of the mayonnaise with the olives. Spread the mixture onto four slices of bread along with the zucchini, provolone, and peppers. op with the slices of bread and coat the outside of the bread with the rest of the mayo mixture.
3. In a non-stick skillet - prepare the sandwiches and cook for approximately 4 minutes (flipping only once).

# Greek Kale Salad with Quinoa Chicken

Makes 2 Servings

*Ingredients*
- 4 c. chopped kale
- 1 ½ c. shredded cooked chicken
- 1 c. cooked quinoa
- ¼ c. of each:
  - Greek salad dressing
  - Jarred – sliced roasted red peppers
- Optional: Crumbled feta cheese

*Directions*
1. Chop the kale and shred the chicken. Add the roasted peppers and quinoa using a large serving dish.
2. Toss well to coat and garnish with the feta.

## Greek Orzo Salad
Makes 8 Servings

*Ingredients*
- 1 c. uncooked orzo pasta
- 6 t. canola/olive oil – divided
- ½ c. minced fresh parsley
- 1 med. finely chopped onion
- 1 ½ t. dried oregano
- 1/3 c. cider/red wine vinegar
- Salt to taste

*Directions*
1. Prepare and drain the orzo. Add it to a serving dish with two teaspoons of the oil.
2. In another dish combine the parsley, onion, salt, vinegar, sugar, rest of the oil, oregano, and pepper. Pour over the orzo and place in the fridge two to 24 hours.
3. Right before the time for lunch, blend in the olives, tomatoes, cucumber, and cheese. Place in the serving dishes and enjoy!

## Lemon & Egg Greek Soup

Makes 8 to 10 servings

*Ingredients*
- ¼ c. converted rice
- ½ t. pepper
- 2 beaten eggs
- 6 c. chicken stock
- 1 t. salt
- Juice of 1 lemon

*Directions*
1. Bring the chicken stock to a simmer in a large pot. Blend in the rice and cook for 15 minutes.
2. Mix the lemon juice and eggs—slowly adding to the simmering broth. Don't boil to prevent curdling. The egg cooks instantly.
3. Flavor with pepper and salt.

# Mediterranean Chicken Quinoa Bowl
Makes 4 Servings

*Ingredients*
- 1 lb. chicken breasts
- 1 jar (7 oz.) roasted red peppers
- ¼ t. each of salt and pepper
- ¼ c. slivered almonds
- 1 small minced garlic clove
- 4 tbsp. olive oil
- 1 t. paprika
- Optional: ¼ t. crushed red pepper
- ½ t. ground cumin
- 2 c. cooked quinoa
- ¼ c. of each chopped:
  - Red onion
  - Kalamata olives – pitted
  - Crumbled feta cheese
- 1 c. diced cucumber
- 2 tbsp freshly chopped parsley
- Also Needed: Rimmed baking pan

*Directions*
1. Remove the bones and skin from the chicken.
2. Prepare the oven broiler (high) and line the baking sheet with aluminum foil.
3. Give the chicken a dusting with the pepper and salt. Arrange on the baking pan and broil for 14-18 minutes, turning once. The thickest part should read 165ºF on the meat thermometer. Transfer to a cutting board to shred or slice.
4. Add the almonds, peppers, 2 tbsp. oil, paprika, crushed red pepper, cumin, and garlic to a

mini food processor. Puree until creamy.

5. Mix the olives, quinoa, rest of the oil, and red onion in a medium dish.

6. Serve by adding the quinoa mixture with cucumber, chicken, and the pepper sauce. Give it a sprinkle of parsley and feta. Smile!

## Mediterranean Tuna
Makes 6 Servings

*Ingredients*
- ¼ c. of each:
  - Drained & chopped roasted red peppers
  - Chopped pitted ripe olives
  - Hellmann's Mayonnaise with olive oil – or a similar product
- 2 sliced green onions
- 1 tbsp. capers – rinsed & drained
- 6 slices bread – whole wheat

*Directions*
1. Mix all of the ingredients into a dish and stir.
2. Serve the tuna on bread or on some greens.

# Mediterranean Tuna Antipasto Salad
Makes 4 Servings

*Ingredients*
- 1 can (15-19-oz.) beans – ex. kidney or chickpeas
- 2 cans (5-6 oz.) water-packed chunk light tuna
- 1 large red bell pepper
- ½ c. of each – diced:
  - Red onion
  - Fresh parsley – divided
- 4 t. rinsed capers
- 1 ½ t. freshly chopped rosemary
- ½ c. lemon juice – divided
- 4 tbsp. olive oil – divided
- ¼ t. salt
- Black pepper to taste
- 8 c. mixed salad greens

*Directions*
1. This is so simple. Drain the beans and tuna. Dice or chop the veggies.
2. Add the ingredients together and serve on top of the salad greens.

## Sesame Tuna Salad
Makes 4 Servings

*Ingredients*
- 1 tbsp. toasted sesame oil
- 3 tbsp. canola oil
- ¼ c. lemon juice/rice vinegar
- 2 tbsp. soy sauce reduced-sodium
- 1 ½ t. of each:
  - Sugar
  - Minced fresh ginger
- 2 cans (5-6 oz. ea.) water-packed chunk light tuna
- 2 sliced scallions
- 1 c. sugar snap/snow peas
- 6 c. thinly sliced cabbage
- 4 sliced/julienne radishes
- ¼ c. fresh cilantro leaves
- 1 t. sesame seeds
- Pepper to taste

*Directions*
1. Whisk the canola oil, lemon juice, soy sauce, sugar, sesame oil, and ginger in a small mixing container.
2. Mix 3 tbsp. of the dressing with the scallions, beans, and tuna in another bowl.
3. Prepare the four Bowls: Add about ½ cup of the tuna mixture onto the bowl. Top it off with the radishes, cilantro, and sesame seeds.
4. Drizzle with the dressing and a shake of pepper to your liking.

## Shrimp Salad Cucumber Cups

Makes 18 Servings

*Ingredients*
- 1 t. minced garlic
- 2 tbsp. minced capers
- 2 tbsp. of each:
    - Chopped parsley
    - Lemon juice
- ¼ c. EVOO
- ½ lb. cooked shrimp (+) 8-10 extra for garnish
- Pepper and salt to taste
- 2 (1 1/3 lb.) English cucumbers – 1 ½ - inches wide

*Directions*
1. Whisk the juice, olive oil, drained capers, garlic, and parsley together in a mixing container. Blend in the shrimp and sprinkle with the pepper and salt.
2. Slice the cucumbers into ¾ - inch slices (18). Scoop out about ½ of the middle and fill with the shrimp salad. Add a shrimp on the top.
3. Serve and enjoy!

## Shrimp Scampi

Makes 4 Servings

*Ingredients*
- 2 tbsp. olive oil (+) more as needed
- 1.5 lb. large shrimp
- Pepper and salt to taste
- 3 minced cloves of garlic
- Large pinch - crushed red pepper flakes
- 4 tbsp. unsalted butter – 4 pieces
- ½ c. dry white wine
- 1 zested lemon
- Optional: Large handful chopped flat-leaf parsley

*Directions*
1. Peel and devein the shrimp – pat dry. Zest and cut the lemon in half – lengthwise and one-half into wedges.
2. Prepare the oil by warming it in a skillet for a minute or so. Toss in the pepper and salt and add the shrimp. Cook for one minute until pink, flip and cook about one more minute. Add to a plate and set aside for now.
3. Lower the heat (medium) and add the pepper flakes, garlic, and a bit of oil. Saute about one minute and add the wine. Simmer and remove the browned bits (they are tasty).
4. Serve with the lemon wedges and enjoy!

# Tasty Gyros with Tzatziki Sauce
Makes 4 Servings

*Ingredients*
- 4 chicken breasts
- ½ red onion
- 1 red pepper
- 1 tbsp. Mediterranean/Italian seasoning
- 4 pitas
- *Optional:*
    - Lettuce
    - Crumbled feta cheese

*Tzatziki Sauce Ingredients*
- 2 c. plain Greek yogurt
- ½ English cucumber
- 1.5 tbsp. lemon juice
- 4 t. minced garlic
- 1/3 c. fresh/frozen dill
- 1/8 t. black pepper
- ½ t. salt – to taste

*Directions*
1. Use a meat tenderizer (or covered hammer) to pound the chicken breast meat to ½-inch thickness. Cut the onions and peppers into thin slices. Peel and dice the cucumber. Chop the dill.
2. Use a food processor or blender and puree the tzatziki sauce. Chill overnight or a minimum of several hours before serving, so the flavors can blend well.
3. Use the Mediterranean or Italian seasoning for

the breasts and cook on the medium setting for five to six minutes for each side. Slice into strips.

4. Stuff the pitas with the pepper strips, lettuce, onions, and chicken.

5. Drizzle the sauce and add the feta. Fold or roll the pita and enjoy. If you like a thicker sauce, just squeeze or pat-dry the cucumbers as much as possible to remove any liquid or juices.

# Two Bean Greek Salad

Makes 4 Servings

*Ingredients*
- 4 ½ t. olive oil - divided
- 1 bag (10-oz.) frozen lima beans or edamame
- ½ t. ground black pepper - divided
- 3 t. fresh chopped oregano - divided
- 2 tbsp. red wine vinegar
- 2 t. Dijon mustard
- ¾ lb. string beans
- 1 c. halved grape tomatoes
- 3 oz. Ricotta Salata or Halloumi cheese
- 2 multigrain pitas
- ¼ c. pitted- halved Kalamata olives
- 1 c. grape tomatoes

*Directions*
1. Slice the cheese into four pieces. Cut the tomatoes and pitas (horizontally) in half. Blend the Dijon mustard, vinegar, 2 teaspoons olive oil, ¼ teaspoon of pepper, and 2 ½ teaspoons oregano in a small serving dish. Place it aside.
2. Add a steamer basket into a saucepan with several inches of water, and cook the beans about three minutes covered. Remove them and put in a dish.
3. Put the string beans into the steamer then cover and cook for about two minutes.
4. Combine the ingredients- adding the olives and tomatoes. Toss the mixture and combine.
5. Serve and top with the bean salad and cheese. Sprinkle the top of the finished product with the rest of the oil.

## Vegan Buddha Bowl
Makes 4 Servings

*Ingredients*
- 1 med. sweet potato
- 3 tbsp. olive oil – divided
- ½ t. divided of each:
  - Salt
  - Black pepper
- 2 tbsp. of each:
  - Water
  - Tahini
- 1 tbsp. lemon juice
- 2 c. quinoa
- 1 small minced clove of garlic
- 1 can rinsed (15 oz.) chickpeas
- 1 firm diced avocado
- ¼ c. freshly chopped cilantro/parsley

*Directions*
1. Set the oven temperature to 425ºF.
2. Combine the potato with 1 tbsp. of oil and ¼ t. of the pepper and salt in a medium mixing container.
3. Add the mixture to a rimmed baking tin. Roast – flipping once - about 15-18 minutes.
4. Whisk the rest of the ingredients in a small dish.
5. Divide the quinoa into the serving dishes with the potatoes, avocado, and chickpeas.
6. Give it a drizzle of the sauce and a sprinkle of cilantro or parsley.
7. Serve and enjoy!

# Chapter 8
## Sides & Just Veggies

## Balsamic Berry Vinaigrette Winter Salad
Makes 8 Servings

*Vinaigrette Ingredients*
- 2 tbsp. plain fat-free Greek yogurt
- ¼ c. balsamic vinegar
- 1 ½ t. olive oil
- 1 tbsp. sugar-free strawberry preserves
- 1 t. Dijon mustard
- ¼ t. kosher salt
- 1 minced garlic clove
- 1/8 t. black pepper

*Other Ingredients*
- 3 c. of each:
  - Torn romaine lettuce
  - Baby spinach
- 1 small cooking apple – ex. Gala
- ½ c. of each:
  - Pomegranate seeds
  - Crumbled boat/blue cheese
- ¼ c. chopped toasted walnuts

*Directions*
1. Prepare the vinaigrette.
2. In another container, combine the romaine, spinach, cheese, apple, walnuts, and pomegranate seeds.
3. Drizzle with the vinaigrette and gently toss. Serve.

# Broccoli – Chickpea & Pomegranate Salad
Makes 6 Servings

*Ingredients*
- ¼ c. red onion
- 1/3 c. whole-milk plain yogurt
- 2 tbsp. of each:
    - Tahini
    - Olive oil
- ½ t. (ground) of each:
    - Pepper
    - Cumin
- ¾ t. salt – divided
- 4 c. (8 oz.) bite-sized broccoli florets
- 1 tbsp. lemon juice
- ½ c. pomegranate seeds
- 1 can (15 oz.) rinsed low-sodium chickpeas

*Directions*
1. Soak the thin onion slices in a dish of cold water for ten minutes and drain.
2. Toast the cumin in a dry skillet (med. heat) for about 1-2 minutes. Pour into a mixing dish along with the tahini, yogurt, pepper, ½ t. salt, lemon juice, and extra-virgin oil. Whisk until creamy.
3. Toss in the chickpeas, broccoli florets, onion, and pomegranate seeds.
4. Let the mixture rest together for about ten minutes to absorb the flavors.
5. Shake in the remainder of the salt. Toss and serve.

## Brussels Sprouts With Honey Pomegranate and Apples

Makes 4 Servings

*Ingredients*
- 1 large Granny Smith apple
- 1 lb. brussels sprouts
- 1 diced med. onion
- 4 tbsp. oil
- ½ c. whole grain freekeh
- ¼ c. dried cranberries
- 2 tbsp. honey
- ¼ - 1/3 finely chopped parsley
- Juice of ½ med. lemon
- Arils (sometimes called arillus) of ½ large pomegranate
- Black pepper
- ¼ t. salt

*Directions*
1. Warm up the oven to 400ºF. Use parchment paper to prepare a cookie sheet.
2. Peel, core, and dice the apple. Also, remove the outer leaves of the sprouts (peel) and cut in half if they are large.
3. Bring 1 ½ cups of water to boil in a small pan, and toss in the freekeh.
4. Let the ingredients in the pan once again come to a boil. Lower the temperature setting to simmer - covered - for twenty to twenty-five minutes which will provide you with 1 ½ cups of the finished product. Take it from the burner and let it rest for five minutes. Drain out the rest of the water.

5. Combine 1/8 teaspoon salt and 2 tablespoons of oil with the sprouts and put them onto the baking sheet for approximately twenty minutes, flipping once after 15 minutes or until they are the desired consistency. Set the sprouts to the side.
6. Using the low-medium setting, use a large sauté pan with two tablespoons of oil, adding the onions for a few minutes. (Don't caramelize the onions.)
7. Combine the lemon juice and apple with the onions and sauté a few more minutes being careful not to let them get soft and mushy.
8. Toss in 1/8 teaspoon of salt, honey, and some pepper; continue to sauté for several minutes.
9. Combine the sprouts and freekeh to the pan and heat everything for several minutes to warm—not hot.
10. Remove from the burner and toss in the parsley, pomegranate seeds, cranberries, pepper, and salt.
11. Enjoy it at room temperature or warmed.
12. Note: If you wish, you can prepare the freekeh and sprouts several days in advance if stored in an air-tight container.

## Greek Salad & Avocado
Makes 8 to 10 Servings

*Ingredients*
- 1 ½ lb. small tomatoes
- 2 English cucumbers
- ¼ cup Italian flat leaf parsley
- 1 1/2 c. – pitted and halved – Kalamata olives
- ½ red onion
- ½ c. each:
  - Olive oil
  - Red wine vinegar
- 2 minced cloves of garlic
- 1 tbsp. oregano
- 1 t. each:
  - Freshly cracked black pepper
  - Kosher salt
- 2 t. sugar

*Directions*
1. Peel the cucumbers into strips and cut into ½-inch slices. Slice the onions and chop the parsley. Also, add the tomatoes and olives into a large serving dish along with the other veggies.
2. Pit and cut the avocado into chunks and set aside for now.
3. Combine the garlic, oregano, red wine, oil, pepper, salt, and sugar into a small Mason jar. Secure the lid and shake well.
4. Pour about one tablespoon of the dressing over the avocado and the remainder over the cucumber mix. Garnish with some feta chunks and bits of avocado.

# Grilled Zucchini - Tomato & Feta
Makes 6 Servings

*Ingredients*
- 3 zucchini/yellow squash or mixture
- ½ t. garlic powder
- Pepper & Salt to taste
- Olive oil
- 1 tbsp. freshly squeezed lemon
- Zest of 1 whole lemon
- 3 pearl tomatoes – chopped - drained
- ½ c. feta cheese
- 1 green onion – white and green parts chopped

*Directions*
1. Warm up the grill ahead of time.
2. Remove the tops and slice the zucchini into halves- lengthwise. Flavor with the garlic powder, pepper, and salt.
3. Drizzle with the extra-virgin olive oil and toss. Prepare on the grill about 3-4 minutes for each side until charred.
4. Add the prepared zucchini to a serving platter and sprinkle with more oil, the zest, and lemon juice. Top with the tomatoes, onions, and feta.
5. Enjoy hot or at room temperature.

# Herbed Mashed Potatoes with Greek Yogurt

Makes 10 to 12 Servings

*Ingredients*
- 4 lb. yellow potatoes
- 1 c. Greek yogurt (whole milk)
- ¼ t. pepper
- 2 t. kosher salt (divided – more or less)
- 1/3 c. each chopped:
  - Chives
  - Dill
  - Parsley
- 3 tbsp. softened butter (divided)
- 1 c. warm milk

*Ingredients for the Toppings*:
- 2 tbsp. of each chopped:
  - Dill
  - Chives
  - Parsley

*Directions*
1. Yukon gold (thin-skinned) potatoes will be used in this recipe; begin by peeling and cutting them into one-inch chunks.
2. Place enough water and one tsp. of salt into a soup pot or a similar pot to cover the potatoes. Put the stove on the highest setting and boil the potatoes. Lower to the medium setting, and boil for about 15 minutes.
3. Turn off the burner, drain the potatoes, and place them back into the pot.
4. Combine 1/2 teaspoon salt, the yogurt, and 1/3

each of the dill, parsley, and chives. Set to the side.

5. Break up the hot potatoes with a potato masher.
6. Combine 2 tablespoons of butter, milk, the pepper, and ½ teaspoon salt. Mash the potatoes until fluffy.
7. Blend the yogurt into the potatoes.
8. Add to the serving dish, and garnish with the butter that remains, with the chopped herbs.

## Mediterranean Bean Salad

Makes 4 Servings

*Ingredients*
- 1 can of each:
    - 15 oz. kidney beans
    - 15.5 oz. garbanzo beans
- 1 lemon – juiced and zested
- 1 med. tomato
- ¼ c. red onion
- ½ c. fresh parsley
- 1 t capers
- 3 tbsp. olive oil
- ½ t. salt to taste

*Directions*
1. Rinse and drain the capers and beans. Chop the onion, tomato, and parsley. Combine all of the ingredients in a large salad bowl and cover.
2. Let it chill about two hours. Stir and serve.

## Roasted Peppers, Olives, and Feta

Makes 6 Servings

*Ingredients*
- 1 each yellow and red pepper
- 1 Vidalia onion
- 8 oz. feta cheese
- 1 head garlic
- 1 t. olive oil
- 1 tbsp. regular capers/8 caper berries
- 12 green olives
- 8 anchovies
- 12 Kalamata olives - pitted
- Juice of 1 lemon
- ¼ cup each:
  - Chives
  - Mint
  - Dill
  - Fresh parsley

*Directions*
1. Slice the peppers into halves, lengthwise. Separate the cloves and peel. Slice the onion into rounds.
2. Preheat the oven to 400ºF.
3. Using a baking sheet, arrange the garlic, onion, and peppers while brushing them with some oil and bake for approximately twenty minutes.
4. Take them from the oven, and place the veggies on a covered dish or under some tight-fitting wrap.
5. Reset the broiler setting on the oven.
6. Use a baking sheet or casserole dish to

crumble the feta. Broil until it bubbles, approximately two minutes.

7. Blend the remainder of the ingredients in a large mixing dish. Combine the onions, garlic, and peppers, tossing well.

8. Take the cheese from the broiler and spoon into the serving plates.

9. Garnish with the pepper mixture.

# Chapter 9
## Dinnertime Favorites

## Broiled Salmon
Makes 4 servings

*Ingredients*
- 4 (5-oz.) salmon fillets
- 15 garlic cloves (divided)
- Pepper and salt
- 1/3 c. olive oil (+ more for the drizzle)
- 2 summer squash
- 2-3 t. dried thyme
- 2 large green onions (white and green parts)
- 1 large tomato
- 1 t. paprika
- 4 tbsp. melted unsalted butter
- ½ c. chopped fresh parsley leaves
- Juice of 1 large lemon or lime
- Lemon wedges for serving

*Directions*
1. Cut four sheets of foil into 12-inch x 17-inch pieces.
2. Warm up the oven to 400ºF.
3. You can use any kind of squash. Cut the squash and tomato in half and slice the onions. Prepare the parsley by removing the stems. Crush and finely chop the garlic cloves.
4. Drizzle some of the olive oil over each one of the fillets, placing the oiled side down onto the foil.
5. Spread half of the prepared garlic over the

salmon and flavor with the dried thyme, pepper, and salt.

6. Combine the melted butter, garlic, pepper, salt, 1/3 cup olive oil, and paprika in a small mixing container.

7. Place one-quarter of the veggies into portions over the fillets. Crimp the foil over them, cover, and seal.

8. Put the packets on a large baking sheet and cook for 20 to 25 minutes.

9. Open each package carefully, so you don't get burned and serve with some lemon wedges.

# Chickpea Patties

Makes 4 Servings

*Ingredients*
- ½ c. flat-leaf fresh parsley
- 1 can 15.5 oz. - chickpeas
- ¼ t. cumin
- 1 garlic clove
- 1 whisked egg
- ½ t. divided of each:
    - Kosher salt
    - Black pepper
- ½ c. low-fat Greek-style yogurt
- 4 tbsp. (divided) all-purpose flour
- 2 tbsp. oil
- 8 c. mixed salad greens
- 3 tbsp. lemon juice
- 1 small red onion
- 1 cup grape tomatoes
- Pita chips - optional

*Directions*
1. Warm some oil in a skillet.
2. Chop the garlic clove, cut the tomatoes in half, and cut the red onion into thin slices.
3. Rinse and drain the chickpeas.
4. Use a food processor to pulp the first four ingredients (parsley, chickpeas, cumin, garlic clove) and add ¼ teaspoon each of the pepper and salt until the mixture is chopped coarsely and holds form.
5. Place the mixture in a bowl and blend the egg and two tablespoons of the flour. Make ½-inch patties. Roll the patties in the rest of the flour.

6. Set the stove on medium-high heat and arrange the patties into the prepared pan, and cook each side for two to three minutes.
7. Whisk the lemon juice, yogurt, and the rest of the pepper together along with the salt.
8. Divide the onions, greens, tomatoes, and patties and sprinkle with about two tablespoons of the dressing over each of the salads.
9. Add pita chips on the side.

# Grilled Chicken & Roasted Pepper Panini
Makes 4 Servings

*Ingredients*
- 1 lb. chicken breast
- ½ t. minced rosemary
- ¼ c. balsamic vinegar
- 1 garlic clove (+) 1 minced
- 1 t. sugar
- ¼ t. red pepper flakes
- 2 tbsp. mayonnaise
- 1 tbsp. olive oil
- 8 (½ oz.) slices of each:
    - Sourdough/French bread
    - Fresh Fontina/mozzarella cheese
- ½ c. roasted fresh roasted bell peppers
- 8 basil leaves

*Directions*
1. Combine the chicken with the vinegar, ½ of the garlic/ rosemary, pepper flakes, 1 tbsp. olive oil, and sugar. Toss well. Marinate in the refrigerator for 30 minutes to two hours.
2. Warm up the oven ahead of time (350ºF). When hot, bake the chicken for 20 minutes (until the pinkish color of the meat is gone). Let it rest for five minutes and then cut into ½-inch slices.
3. Mix the rest of the garlic and mayo. Spread ½ tbsp. of the mixture on the (unoiled) side of the bread slices. Layer the cheese with 2 tbsp. of peppers, 2 basil leaves and ¼ of the chicken slices.

4. Top the sandwich with another slice of bread. Lightly spray the sandwich with some olive oil spray.
5. Use a grill pan (med-hi) and add the sandwiches. Place a heavy item on top to hold them in place (5 min. per side). Serve.

# Grilled Lamb Chops and Mint

Makes 6 Servings

*Ingredients*
- ¼ t. red pepper flakes
- ½ c. chopped mint leaves (+) more for garnish
- Sea salt
- 1/3 c. olive oil
- 2 smashed cloves garlic
- 12 small rib lamb chops - 2 1/3 lbs. approx.

*Directions*
1. Set the grill's heat to medium-high.
2. Blend the red pepper flakes, olive oil, salt, and mint in a mixing container.
3. Rub the lamb chops with the garlic.
4. Add a few tablespoons of the mint in a container to cover the lamb. Grill the chops approximately 3-4 minutes on both sides or until charred. (Note: You can achieve a medium rare consistency when you push down on the center of the chop, and it is somewhat firm.)
5. Put the chops on a serving dish and brush with the remainder of the mint oil mixture. Garnish with some bits of mint.

## Hassel-back Caprese Chicken

Makes 4 Servings

*Ingredients*
- 2 (8 oz. ea.) chicken breasts
- ½ t. each – divided: Pepper and salt
- 1 med. sliced tomato
- ¼ c. prepared pesto
- 3 oz. fresh mozzarella
- 8 c. broccoli florets
- 2 tbsp. EVOO
- Also Needed: Large rimmed baking sheet

*Directions*
1. Remove the bones and skins from the chicken.
2. Set the oven temperature to 375ºF. Prepare the baking pan with cooking spray.
3. Slice the chicken with ½-inch crossways cuts – almost to the bottom – but not completely through.
4. Season with the pepper and salt then fill with the tomato and mozzarella slices. Brush with the pesto and add to the baking tray.
5. Toss the broccoli in oil and the rest of the pepper and salt. Add to the other side of the baking tin. Prepare for 25 minutes (make sure the inside isn't pink).
6. Slice the chicken into halves and enjoy it with the broccoli.

# Lamb Lettuce Wraps

Makes 4 Servings

*Ingredients*
- 1 c. onion
- 2 t. canola oil
- 1 t. ground cinnamon
- 2 t. minced garlic
- ¼ t. freshly cracked black pepper
- ¾ t. kosher salt
- ½ c. chopped of each:
  - Fresh parsley
  - Cucumber
  - Tomato
- ¼ c. Greek yogurt – plain fat-free
- ¼ c. red pepper hummus – ex. Tribe
- 8 lettuce leaves
- 1 tbsp. toasted pine nuts
- 2 tbsp. torn mint leaves
- 6 oz. lean ground lamb

*Directions*
1. Dial the stove's heat to the highest setting and warm up the oil in a frying pan. Toss in the finely chopped onions, garlic, salt, cinnamon, and pepper along with the lamb. Saute until done, or about five minutes.
2. Mix the cucumber, tomato, and parsley in a mixing container. Stir in the lamb mixture. Mix the hummus and yogurt in another dish.
3. Arrange about ¼ of the cooked lamb in each of the lettuce leaves.
4. Top each one off with a tablespoon of the hummus mixture and garnish.

# Lamb with Garlic & Rosemary

Makes 4 Servings

*Ingredients*
- 1 lb. boneless leg of lamb (3/4-inch cubes)
- 4 (6-inch) whole wheat pitas
- 1 container plain low-fat yogurt - (6-oz.)
- 1 t. minced garlic (bottled)
- ¼ (+) 1/8 t. black pepper
- ½ t. salt - divided
- 1 tbsp. fresh chopped rosemary
- 2 t. olive oil
- 1 ½ c. seeded cucumber
- 1 tbsp. lemon juice

*Directions*
1. Set the stove's heat to medium-high to warm up the oil in a large pan.
2. Combine the rosemary, garlic, ¼ teaspoon each of salt and pepper, as well as the lamb as you toss and coat it.
3. Place the mixture into the pan and sauté for four minutes.
4. Meanwhile, combine ¼ teaspoon salt, the lemon juice, finely chopped cucumber, yogurt, and 1/8 tsp. of black pepper.
5. Place the lamb mixture into the pitas and drizzle with the prepared sauce.

# Lemon - Za'atar - Grilled Chicken
Makes 4 Servings

*Ingredients*
- 4 chicken thighs - 6-8 oz. ea.
- 1 t. lemon zest
- 1 sliced lemon wedges
- 2 tbsp. lemon juice
- 8 green onions
- 1 t. minced cloves of garlic
- ¼ t. of each:
  - Salt
  - Pepper

*Directions*
1. Blend the zest, oil, lemon juice, za'atar, pepper, garlic, and salt in a big container. Put the thighs into the mix and fully cover the surfaces.
2. Use the medium grill temperature setting ranging from 350ºF to 450ºF. Arrange the chicken on the surface—skin side down—for 5-8 minutes. Flip the thighs and cook for approximately four additional minutes.
3. For the last few minutes, grill the onions and lemon wedges—flipping once.
4. *Note*: The za'atar for this recipe can be located in the Middle Eastern section of most superstores.

# Lemony Salmon & Lima Beans

Makes 4 Servings

*Ingredients*
- 4 center-cut (5 oz.) skinless salmon fillets
- 1 lb. frozen baby lima beans
- ½ c. nonfat plain Greek yogurt
- 1 lemon
- ¾ t. paprika
- 3 thinly sliced cloves garlic
- 1 ½ c. of water
- Pinch of red pepper flakes
- ¾ t. dried oregano
- Black pepper
- Kosher salt
- 2 tbsp. fresh chopped parsley
- 2 t. olive oil

*Directions*
1. Prepare the oven using the broiler function.
2. Cover a cookie sheet with foil. Put one teaspoon of the oil in a medium saucepan and preheat.
3. For ½ of the lemon, slice it into four thin rounds. Using a grater make the zest and set it to the side for later.
4. Combine some of the juice in a dish, add ¼ teaspoon of the paprika and the yogurt.
5. Place the garlic, oregano, and red pepper flakes in the pan and cook approximately two minutes. Add the water, beans, and lemon zest. Simmer for approximately 20 minutes. Flavor the mixture with the pepper and salt if desired. Take the pan off the burner and add

one tablespoon of the paprika-yogurt mixture, parsley, and rest of the oil.

6. In a small dish, combine ½ teaspoon of the salt, ½ teaspoon of paprika, and pepper if desired. Add by drizzling over the salmon.

7. Place the salmon on the prepared pan and top each of the salmon fillets with a slice of lemon.

8. Broil for about six to eight minutes. Enjoy the salmon with the lima beans and garnish with the paprika-yogurt mixture.

# Rigatoni with Asiago Cheese & Green Olive-Almond Pesto

Makes 6 Servings

*Ingredients*
- ½ c. fresh flat-leaf parsley leaves
- 1 ¼ c. green olives
- 1 lb. uncooked rigatoni
- 2 tbsp. water
- ½ c. of each:
  - Grated Asiago cheese – 2 oz. approx.
  - Sliced toasted almonds
- 1 t. white wine vinegar
- 1 large clove of garlic
- ¼ t. black pepper

*Directions*
1. Prepare the rigatoni using the package instructions (remove the fat and salt), and drain. Reserve 6 tbsp. of the liquid.
2. Use a food processor, and add the sliced almonds, olives, parsley leaves, garlic, and black pepper. Pulp the ingredients until they reach a coarsely chopped consistency (pulp about 3 times).
3. Leave the processor on, and add 1 teaspoon vinegar and 2 tablespoons of water. Pulp until the ingredients are finely chopped.
4. Mix the olive combination and ¼ cup of the reserved liquids, as well as the pasta, in a large mixing dish - tossing well.
5. Add only enough of the remainder of the liquid to make the pasta maintain its moist consistency. Sprinkle with the cheese and serve.

## Salmon Rice Bowl

Makes 4 Servings

*Ingredients*
- 2 med. gold beets
- 1 c. wild rice blend
- 8 oz. Brussels sprouts
- 3 tbsp. olive oil – divided
- ¾ t. salt – divided
- ¾ t. ground black pepper – divided
- 1 lb. wild-caught salmon
- 1 lemon
- 2 rosemary sprigs
- 1 minced garlic clove
- 2 tbsp herbs – ex. basil, rosemary, thyme, etc.
- 1 tbsp. chopped pistachios
- Also Needed: Deep baking sheet

*Directions*
1. Warm up the oven to 425ºF.
2. Trim the veggies. Slice the beets into ½ - inch wedges. Slice the salmon into four portions. Chop the herbs and mince the garlic.
3. Toss the sprouts and beets into a dish with one tablespoon of the oil along with the salt and pepper.
4. Prepare the rice and let it cool for about ten minutes. Spread out the veggies on a baking sheet and roast (15 min.).
5. Slice the lemon in half – slice ½ crosswise and into slices. Save the other half for later.
6. Sprinkle the salmon with salt and pepper. Add a rosemary sprig and a lemon slice. Roast until the veggies are softened (9-12 min.).

7. Freshly squeeze the lemon into a dish. Whisk in the rest of the oil (2 tbsp.) herbs, salt, and pepper.
8. Divide and serve. Trash the rosemary sprig and lemon slices. Serve the salmon with the veggies and rice.

## Seared Tuna Steaks
Makes 4 Servings

*Ingredients*
- 1/8 t. black pepper
- ½ t. of each:
- Ground coriander
- Salt -divided
- 4 (6 oz.) ¾-inch thick Yellow-fin tuna steaks

*Tomato Mixture Ingredients*
- ½t. minced garlic (bottled)
- 12 pitted chopped Kalamata olives
- 1 tbsp. each
    - Olive oil
    - Drained capers
    - Lemon juice
- 3 tbsp. freshly chopped parsley
- ¼ c. green chopped onions
- 1 ½ c. seeded chopped tomatoes

*Directions*
1. Put the stove on medium-high and place a large pan on the stovetop with the cooking spray added.
2. Drizzle the fish with the pepper, coriander, and ¼ teaspoon of salt and add to the pan. Cook four minutes per side.
3. Blend the remainder of the ingredients.
4. Garnish the fish with the tomato mixture and serve.

# Spicy Spinach Lentil Soup

Makes 4-6 Servings

*Ingredients*
- 1 large of each:
  - Clove of garlic
  - Yellow onion
- 2 tbsp. olive oil
- 2 t. dried mint flakes
- 1 ½ t. of each:
  - Crushed red peppers
  - Ground cumin
  - Sumac
  - Ground coriander
- Pinch of sugar
- Pepper and salt to taste
- 1 tbsp. flour
- 3 c. (+) more if needed
- 6 c. - low-sodium vegetable broth
- 12 oz. frozen cut leaf spinach
- 1 ½ c. rinsed small brown lentils
- 2 c. freshly chopped flat leaf parsley
- Juice of 1 lime

*Directions*
1. Warm up the oil in a cast iron or ceramic pot. Toss in the chopped onions, garlic, spices, sugar, flour, and dried mint. Simmer for about two minutes (med-hi) and stir often.
2. Add the water and broth. Change the stove's setting to high-heat and bring it to a rolling boil. Toss in the lentils and *frozen* spinach. Boil for five minutes (high) then lower the heat to

med-low and cover – cook for another 20 minutes.

3. When fully cooked, add the chopped parsley and lime juice. Stir and set the pot aside for about five minutes to let the flavors blend together.

4. Serve with your favorite bread.

# Stuffed Peppers
Makes 4-6 Servings

*Ingredients*
- 1 tbsp. olive oil
- ½ lb. ground beef
- ½ t. of each:
  - Allspice
  - Garlic powder
  - Hot/sweet paprika
- Pepper & Salt to taste
- 1 c. of each:
  - Cooked chickpeas
  - Short-grain rice
- 3 tbsp. tomato sauce
- 2 ¼ c. water
- ¾ c. chicken broth/water
- 6 bell peppers – any color

*Directions*
1. Soak the rice in water for 10-15 minutes then drain. Chop the veggies and core the peppers.
2. Warm up a heavy skillet (med.-high) and add the oil. Sauté the onions until brown and add the black pepper, salt, garlic powder, and allspice.
3. Mix in the chickpeas and stir for a minute or so. Toss in the rice, parsley, tomato sauce, and paprika. Pour in the water and bring it to a boil. Lower the heat by half then change it to the lowest setting. Place a lid on the pot and cook for 15-20 minutes until the rice is fluffy.
4. Warm up a grill to med-high and grill the peppers for 10-15 minutes (lid on). Turn

occasionally. Let it cool and warm up the oven to 350ºF.

5. Prepare the peppers with the open side up. Add the cooked rice mixture to each pepper and arrange in a baking dish filled with the broth or water.

6. Tightly cover the dish and bake 20-30 minutes.

7. Remove and garnish with parsley and serve with a favorite side.

# Chapter 10
## Desserts & Snacks

## Snacks

### Basil & Tomato Finger Sandwiches
Makes 4 Servings

*Ingredients*
- 4 slices of bread – whole wheat
- 8 t. mayonnaise reduced-fat – divided
- 4 t. fresh basil
- 4 thick slices of tomato
- 1/8 t. each of salt and pepper

*Directions*
1. Remove the edges from the bread to a size that's a little larger than the tomato.
2. Add the mayo and top with the tomato, pepper, salt, and basil.
3. Close and enjoy!

# Cherries – Toasted Almonds and Ricotta

Makes 1 Serving

## *Ingredients*

- 1 tbsp. toasted slivered almonds
- 1/3 c. pitted frozen cherries
- 2 tbsp. ricotta - part-skim

## *Directions*

1. Warm up the cherries for 1-2 minutes using the high-setting in the microwave.
2. Scoop the ricotta and almonds on top and enjoy!

# Cranberry, Goat Cheese, and Walnut Canapés
Makes 8 Servings

*Ingredients*
- 24 thin slices baguette - whole wheat
- ¾ c. (approx. 24 halves) walnuts
- 1/8 t. ground cinnamon
- Ground pepper and coarse salt
- 4 t. olive oil
- ½ c. dried cranberries
- 8 oz. fresh goat cheese
- 2 tbsp. water
- 1 t. fresh chopped thyme (+) leaves for garnishing

*Directions*
1. Warm up the oven temperature to 375ºF.
2. Use a baking sheet with high sides, and add 1 teaspoon of oil, salt, pepper, and cinnamon. Toss in the nuts. Bake for 4 to 6 minutes. Set to the side.
3. Using the same sheet, place the baguette slices and brush with oil - flavoring it with pepper and salt.
4. Bake for 10 to 15 minutes. Rotate the pan halfway through the cooking process.
5. In a medium bowl, blend the water with the cheese. Mix in the thyme and cranberries with a dash of pepper or salt.
6. Serve the goat cheese with the slices of bread. Garnish each one with thyme leaves and a few walnuts.

## Creamy Blueberries
Makes 4 Servings

*Ingredients*
- 4 oz. reduced-fat cream cheese
- ¾ c. low-fat vanilla yogurt
- 2 t. lemon zest
- 1 t. honey
- 2 c. fresh blueberries

*Directions*
1. Break the cream cheese apart and add it to a medium mixing dish. Drain the liquid from the yogurt and add to the bowl along with the honey.
2. Mix with a high-speed blender until creamy and stir in the zest.
3. Arrange the cream and berries in layers on the dessert dishes or a fancy wine glass.
4. Enjoy now or place in the fridge to serve later (up to 8 hours).

## Cucumber Roll-Ups

Makes 6 Servings

*Ingredients*
- 1 large cucumber
- 6 tbsp. of each:
    - Roasted chopped red pepper or sun-dried tomatoes
    - Roasted garlic hummus
    - Crumbled feta
- 1/8 t. black pepper

*Directions*
1. Peel or shave the cucumber with a veggie peeler or sharp knife to make thin cucumber slices or slice it with a kitchen knife. Remove the seeds. You should get 12 slices.
2. Sprinkle with a dash of pepper, and add 1 ½ teaspoons each of the hummus, pepper, and feta to each slice.
3. Gently roll the filled cucumber and insert a toothpick in the center to hold it together.
4. Arrange it on the serving platter with the other side facing downwards.

## Date Wraps

Makes 16 Servings

*Ingredients*
- 16 whole pitted dates
- 16 slices prosciutto
- To Taste: Freshly cracked black pepper

*Directions*
1. Use thinly sliced prosciutto and wrap around each date.
2. Grind the pepper on top and serve. Tasty mix!

## Greek Yogurt Parfait

Makes 4 Servings

*Ingredients*
- ¼ c. unsalted dry roasted pistachios
- 3 c. plain yogurt
- 4 t. honey
- 1 t. vanilla extract
- 28 clementine segments

*Directions*
1. Shell and chop the pistachios. Blend the vanilla and yogurt in a dish. (Greek-style fat-free is the best choice.)
2. Spoon approximately 1/3 cup of the yogurt blend into four parfait glasses (the bottom layer). Garnish each with five clementine sections, ½ teaspoon honey, and ½ tablespoon of the nuts.
3. Use the rest of the yogurt mix in each of the cups—topping each off with ½ tablespoon of the nuts, ½ teaspoon of the honey, and 2 each of the clementine sections.

## Herbed Olives
Makes 16 Servings

*Ingredients*
- 2 t. EVOO
- 3 c. olives – your choice
- 1 garlic clove - minced
- 1/8 t. dried of each:
  - Basil
  - Oregano
- Pepper to taste

*Directions*
1. Combine all of the ingredients (pepper, garlic, basil, oregano, oil, and olives) in a medium dish. Toss.
2. Enjoy anytime!

# Dips and Sauces

### Marinated Olives & Feta
Makes 12 Servings

*Ingredients*
- 2 tbsp. olive oil
- ½ c. diced feta cheese
- 1 c. Kalamata/mixed Greek pitted olives
- Zest & juice - 1 lemon
- 2 minced garlic cloves
- 1 t. freshly chopped rosemary
- Pepper to taste
- Pinch crushed red pepper

*Directions*
1. Combine all of the ingredients in a medium serving dish.
2. Cover and place in the fridge for up to one day.

## Picnic Snack
Makes 1 Serving

*Ingredients*
- 10 cherry tomatoes
- 1 slice crusty bread – whole wheat
- ¼ oz. sliced aged cheese
- 6 oil-cured olives

*Directions*
1. For a quick lunch or picnic; toss all of the ingredients into a portable container.
2. Go enjoy your day!

## Tomato & Basil Skewers
Makes 16 Servings

*Ingredients*
- 16 fresh pieces each of:
  - Cherry tomatoes
  - Basil leaves
  - Mozzarella balls
- Drizzle - extra-virgin olive oil
- Ground black pepper & Coarse salt to taste

*Directions*
1. Prepare by skewering the ingredients together.
2. Drizzle with the oil and a shake of pepper and salt.
3. Delicious!

# Conclusion

Thanks for reading your entire copy of the *Mediterranean Diet for Beginners: The Complete Guide To Lose Weight And Live Healthier Following The Mediterranean Lifestyle.* Let's hope it was informative and that it provided you with all of the tools you need to achieve your goals.

As you probably noticed, several key items were mentioned several times because they will play a huge part in the success of your new way of life. The Mediterranean Diet Plan can truly create a healthier future for you and your family if you follow these guidelines.

You will find that you can eat healthier meals and not be hungry. This is not a 'fad' diet plan and has been around for many years in other countries around the Mediterranean locality. The plan offers a huge variety and many wonderful flavors to entice even the pickiest eater.

## Consider these guidelines

- Eat fresh fruit and vegetables daily.
- Use extra-virgin olive oil (EVOO) for

everything in your diet plan.

- Maximize on natural, whole foods versus the completely processed ones
- Eat small amounts of red meat.
- Concentrated sugars should not be eaten more than a few times weekly.
- Consume the bulk of your diet using plant foods; fruits, nuts, beans, potatoes, seeds, and whole wheat products.

One other thing that's worth mentioning as you begin this new life challenge is to think of your local markets. Not only will you be getting the best possible produce; you will be supporting your community by checking your residence to locate areas where farming communities reside. That would be a great way to find someone to share your new adventure with and compare notes. It is always much more fun when you have a partner to enjoy the new challenges offered. This dieting concept is not any different in that aspect.

As you read through your new Mediterranean diet plan, you can rest assured that you have a diet plan you and your family will enjoy.

Finally, if you found this book useful in any way, a review on Amazon is always appreciated!

# Recipes Index In Alphabetical Order

## Other Books By Elizabeth Wells

### Keto Diet For Beginners
Complete Beginner's Guide To Lose Weight Fast And Live Healthier With Ketogenic Cooking

Would you like to lose weight and feel better without only eating salads? Have you already followed countless diets, without actually seeing any results? This one is different, and the results will speak for themselves.

The Ketogenic Diet, or Keto Diet, is a solid dieting

program created back in 1924 by Dr. Russel Wilder and supported by many scientific studies. The Keto Diet is not another diet that promises you everything and delivers you little to nothing! This dieting style lost popularity when some sketchy "lose weight effortlessly" diets came out some years ago, but it is now being acclaimed worldwide again, with famous people following it and new scientific studies being published.

The Keto Diet is based on this principle: your body usually gets energy from the carbs you eat and stores all the excess fats (think about love handles or belly fat). Most diets tell you to stop eating fats to lose weight, however there's a better way to do it.

Some types of fats are healthy and eating them more, while also reducing your intake of carbs, will help you lose weight faster. In fact, if you start eating low carb and high fat your body will use the fats instead of the carbohydrates to produce energy, without actually storing them.

This way, your body will naturally burn fats for you, just by eating the right foods. And the best part is ketogenic foods actually taste really good. Imagine how ketogenic cooking will improve your shape and overall health.

*"Once you have been on the ketogenic diet for a few weeks and begun to experience its benefits you will never want to go back to high-carb eating. After all, ketosis is the body's natural state. It's how we were designed to live."*

Following this diet is easy when you have the right help. That's why this book will teach you **everything you need to know about the keto diet** to help you lose weight fast and feel better, without being too tricky or complicated. You'll learn exactly what to eat, what to avoid, what recipes to cook, what to store in your pantry to follow the keto diet correctly and start improving your health right now.

**Some benefits you'll get by going keto:**

- Lose Weight Fast And In A Natural Way
- Feel Better, Both Mentally And Physically
- Eat Healthy Foods That Actually Taste Good
- Have A Healthy, Younger Looking Skin
- Feel Full Of Energy All Day Long
- Lower Your Triglyceride Levels To Prevent Heart Attacks
- Eat Foods That Won't Leave You Hungry All Day
- Improve Your Physical Performance
- Lower Your Cancer Risk
- And Much, Much More

**In this book you'll learn:**

- What Is The Ketogenic Diet and How It Works
- All The Real Benefits Of The Ketogenic Diet
- A Complete 14-day Keto Meal Plan To Successfully Go Keto
- 20+ Delicious Keto Recipes For Breakfast, Lunch And Dinner
- A List Of Keto Friendly Foods To Store In Your Pantry
- The Complete Keto Shopping List To Fill Your Cart With Healthy Foods
- How To Know If You Shouldn't Follow This Diet
- Simple Tips And Tricks To Stay Keto While

Travelling
- How To Stay On The Keto Diet Through The Holidays
- And Much More

Start improving your health today!

**"Keto Diet For Beginners" by Elizabeth Wells is available at Amazon.**

## Keto Pressure Cooker
101 Delicious Ketogenic Recipes For The Electric Pressure Cooker To Lose Weight Fast And Live Healthier

If you love the ketogenic diet and would like to cook dishes using your electric pressure cooker this book is for you. Cooking keto using an electric pressure cooker will help you save time and money without losing the countless benefits of a high fat, low carb diet.

In this cookbook, you'll find 101 mouthwatering ketogenic recipes for every meal time, breakfast, lunch, dinner, sides and desserts. All the recipes include comprehensive instructions and nutritional values, allowing you to know the amount of calories, fats, carbohydrates and proteins contained in each dish.

With the help of these recipes you will easily transition toward a healthier lifestyle.

**Some recipes you'll find:**
- Korean Steamed Eggs
- Ham And Pepper Fritatta
- Italian Sausage Kale Soup
- Creamy Cauliflower Chowder
- Cream Of Mushroom
- Shredded Chicken
- Green Beans And Bacon
- Prosciutto Wrapped-asparagus
- Coconut Milk Shrimp
- Salmon With Orange Ginger Sauce
- Garlic Cuban Pork
- Garlic And Parmesan Asparagus
- Pumpkin Cheesecake
- Chocolate Mousse
- Coconut Almond Cake
- Chocolate Cheesecake
- And Much More

**Enjoy these keto dishes today!**

**"Keto Pressure Cooker" by Elizabeth Wells is available at Amazon.**

## Keto Slow Cooker
101 Delicious Ketogenic Recipes For The Slow Cooker To Lose Weight Fast And Live Healthier

Are you on a ketogenic diet and would love to cook using your slow cooker? Imagine putting a bunch of ingredients in your slow cooker before going to work and coming home to a delicious keto approved meal.

In this cookbook, you'll find 101 delicious ketogenic recipes you can easily cook with your slow cooker. Just follow the simple steps, put all the ingredients in, and let the slow cooker do the rest. You'll discover recipes for chilis, soups, stews, beef meals, poultry and pork dishes, desserts and other tasty treats that will help you save time without losing the countless benefits of a high fat, low carb diet.

All the recipes include step-by-step instructions and nutritional values, allowing you to know the amount of calories, fats, carbohydrates and proteins contained in each dish. And remember, you don't have to spend your entire day in the kitchen to cook healthy dishes.

**Some recipes you'll find:**
- Chicken Chorizo Soup
- Hare Stew
- BBQ Pulled Beef
- Balsamic Chicken Thighs
- Cuban Ropa Vieja
- Cranberry Pork Roast
- Poached Salmon
- Zucchini Bread
- Chile Verde
- Summertime Veggies
- Jamaican Jerk Roast
- Raspberry Coconut Cake
- Lemon Frosted Cake
- Grain-Free Granola
- And Much More

**Enjoy your new recipes today!**

**"Keto Slow Cooker" by Elizabeth Wells is available at Amazon.**

## Keto Diet For Beginners
The Step By Step Guide For Beginners To Lose Weight Fast And Live Healthier With The Ketogenic Diet

Let's face it, so many people are already in love with this high-fat, low carb diet these days, but there's so much information out there that it can be very overwhelming to figure out how to follow the ketogenic diet without making the most common mistakes.

If you're interested in the keto diet, but don't know where to start, look no further. In this beginner's guide you'll find everything you need to know to start a keto diet and be successful on your dieting journey.

This book will take you step by step through the fundamental principles of the keto diet, will answer all the most common questions and will teach you what foods to eat and what to avoid without being too complicated or overwhelming. After reading this book, you will be well on your way to entering the state known as "ketosis" and jump-starting your new weight loss regimen on the Keto lifestyle.

**In this guide you'll find:**
- A Step-by-step Process To Start A Keto Diet The Right Way
- History And Fundamental Principles Of The Keto Diet
- How The Ketogenic Diet Works And What You Need To Start Today
- A 30-day Meal Plan Template To Guide You With All The Recipes You Need
- 60 Healthy Ketogenic Recipes For Healthy Breakfast, Lunch, Dinner, Desserts, Snacks And Salads
- A Complete List Of Foods You Should And Shouldn't Eat
- All The Health Benefits You'll Get By Going Keto
- How To Avoid The Common Mistakes All Beginners Make While Starting The Keto Diet
- Ketogenic FAQs: Answers To All The Most Common Questions About The Ketogenic Diet

You will learn all about ketogenic, fasting, weight

loss, and how a low-carb, high-protein diet can change your life mentally, physically, and even emotionally. This book covers its origins as a treatment for epilepsy to all the health problems we face in today's highly processed, fast food world, and how this all contributes to our health. Once you decide to begin a ketogenic diet you will be helping yourself against obesity, diabetes, inflammatory diseases, heart health, curbing dementia, and so much more!

You'll learn how to start the Keto diet successfully with a step-by-step process on how to begin, as well as an extensive list of foods that can and cannot be eaten, so you will be able to know from the start exactly what you should be eating. You'll also find a 30-day meal planning guide along with all the recipes so you can begin planning and hop right away, no need to research for recipes!

## Some recipes you'll find in this book:
- Garlic Cedar Plank Salmon
- Prosciutto Wrapped Asparagus
- Tuna Lettuce Wrap With Avocado Yogurt Dressing
- Chicken and Cilantro Salad
- Grilled Salmon with Avocado Bruschetta
- Steak With Balsamic Tomatoes
- California Spicy Crab Stuffed Avocado
- Chicken Pesto Bake
- Zucchini Rolls
- Sausage Stuffed Zucchini with Mozzarella Cheese
- Steak Kebabs with Chimichurri
- Flourless Chocolate Keto Brownies
- Cinnamon Pecan Bars

- Raspberry Lemon Cupcakes
- And Much More

And the best part is, these recipes actually taste good, because remember, being on a diet doesn't have to mean eating flavorless food.

**Start the Keto Diet today!**

**"Keto Diet For Beginners" by Elizabeth Wells is available at Amazon.**

## Keto Diet
### Complete Beginner's Guide To Lose Weight Fast And Live Healthier With Ketogenic Cooking

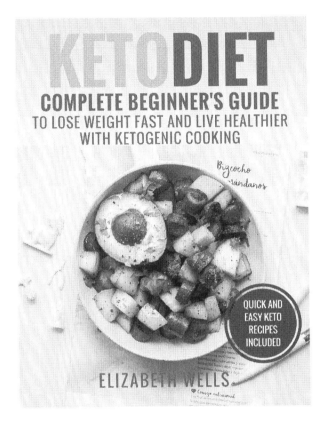

Have you already tried every known diet without seeing any results? Are you willing to lose weight and improve your health but don't want to quit eating some of your loved dishes?

You've come to the right place. The Ketogenic Diet is a popular dieting program that has been around for decades. The Keto Diet is not another fad regime that promises you everything and delivers you little to nothing! This dieting style has been created by Dr. Russell Wilder back in 1924 and is proven and supported by many scientific studies. It lost popularity when some fad "lose weight quick" diets came out some decades ago.

Recently it is being rediscovered and is already acclaimed worldwide. The Keto Diet is well known for being a low carb diet, where the body produces ketones instead of glucose to be used as energy. This will help it burn fats to produce energy without storing them and will drastically reduce the amount of weight you accumulate.

"Eating high fat and low carb offers many health, weight loss, physical and mental performance benefits."

You don't have to quit eating fats to lose weight. You'll still be able to enjoy food that actually tastes good and makes you happy.

In this book you'll learn how the Keto Diet works and how you can start improving your health right now by cooking delicious dishes.

**These are some of the benefits you'll get:**

- Lose weight naturally and easily
- Feel well, both mentally and physically
- Keep your skin younger looking
- Eat healthy foods you actually like
- Satisfy your appetite without remaining hungry all day
- Achieve a lower blood pressure
- Prevent heart attacks by lowering your triglyceride levels
- Increase your energy and improve your physical performance
- Lower your cancer risk

- And much more

Following this diet without any help can be complex, especially if you're a beginner. That's why this book aims to teach you everything you need to know to improve your eating habits and your life, without being too tricky or complicated.

**In this book you'll learn:**

- What is the Ketogenic Diet
- What You Should Eat (And What You Shouldn't)
- 43 Recommended Foods (with calories, grams of carbs, proteins and fats contained)
- How To Follow The Keto Diet Correctly (Most People Get This Wrong)
- 3 Signs That You've Reached Ketosis
- The Benefits Of Going Keto
- 50 Quick And Easy To Cook Keto Recipes
- And much more

What are you waiting for? Start eating healthier today!

**"Keto Diet" by Elizabeth Wells is available at Amazon.**

## Keto Meal Prep
### Complete Beginner's Guide To Save Time And Eat Healthier With Batch Cooking For The Ketogenic Diet

If you're one of the thousands of people on a ketogenic diet you already know and love all its benefits and the amount of energy a low-carb, high-fat diet can give you. Unfortunately, cooking healthy dishes usually takes time, and not everyone can spend 3+ hours in the kitchen every day to cook for breakfast, lunch and dinner. If you're looking for a way to save time while still eating delicious keto approved dishes, this book is for you.

Learning how to plan and cook your meals in advance is one of the best things that you can do. Meal prepping, also known as batch cooking, helps you stay on the ketogenic diet, makes it easy to save time during the week, keeps you away from your temptations, and can even save you a lot of money. And when you combine the ketogenic diet with your meal prepping goals, you are going to lose weight and feel great in no time.

This guidebook is going to provide you with all the tools that you need to get started with meal prepping on the ketogenic diet.

**In this guidebook you'll learn:**
- The Basic Principles Of The Ketogenic Diet
- The Right Way To Start Meal Prepping Today
- How To Avoid The Common Mistakes Made By Meal Prepping Beginners
- 100 Keto Friendly Meal Prep Recipes For Easy Breakfasts, Lunches And Dinners, Snacks And Desserts
- A Complete 30-day Meal Plan To Keep You On Your Goals
- And Much More

**Some of the meal prep recipes you'll find:**
- Keto Monkey Bread
- Roast Beef Cups
- Pork Salad
- Baked Chicken Nuggets
- Pumpkin Soup
- Super Green Soup
- Beef Stew
- Chocolate and Peanut Butter Muffins
- Blender pancakes
- Butter Coffee
- Walnut Bites
- Smoked Salmon and Dill Spread
- Lime and Coconut Fat Bombs
- Low Carb Bars

- Avocado Tropical Treat
- Keto Lava Cake
- And Many Other Recipes

**Save time and eat healthier with meal prepping on a ketogenic diet**

**"Keto Meal Prep" by Elizabeth Wells is available at Amazon.**

## Meal Prep Guide
Discover How To Lose Weight, Spend Less Time In The Kitchen And Eat Healthier With Meal Prepping

Do you work a full-time job or just have a busy lifestyle and find it difficult to prepare a healthy meal every day?

Cooking takes time, and with our busy lives not everybody can spend hours in the kitchen everyday. Meal prepping, also known as batch cooking, is the definitive solution to this problem. By learning how to cook your meals in advance and store them safely you'll be able to easily save time (and money) while still eating healthy, homemade food.

In this book you'll learn all the basics you need to know to start meal prepping your food and store it safely. You'll also find over 70 delicious recipes suitable for meal prepping that will teach you how to cook delicious dishes for your breakfasts, dinners, lunches, desserts, and lunch boxes.

## You'll learn:

- How To Save Time And Cook Healthy Dishes With Meal Prepping
- The Meal Prep Method: How To Prep And Safely Store Eggs, Meat, Grains And Fruits
- 70+ Delicious Recipes To Save Time And Cook Healthy Dishes For Breakfast, Lunch, Dinner And Dessert.
- One-Serving Smoothie Recipes For Healthy Snacks To Enjoy At Any Time Of The Day
- And Much More

With this unique collection of recipes, you will be able to stock your refrigerator with tasty meals and snacks to please everyone in your household.

## Here are some recipes you'll find inside the book:

- Mexican Breakfast Taquitos
- Chickpea & Butternut Fajitas
- Apple Butternut Squash Soup
- Egg Cups
- Black Bean & Sweet Potato Salad
- Southwestern Sweet Potato Lentil Jar Salad
- Cilantro Lime Chicken & Cauliflower Rice
- Green Tropical Bowl
- Almond Butter - Brown Rice Crispy Treats
- Banana Strawberry & Green Smoothie

Stop eating junk food just because you don't have enough time to cook healthy.

**Start meal prepping today!**

**"Meal Prep Guide" by Elizabeth Wells is available at Amazon.**

## Ketogenic Diet Guide For Beginners:

"Ketogenic Diet Guide For Beginners" by Elizabeth Wells is available at Amazon.

Made in the USA
San Bernardino, CA
11 April 2018